CONDOLEEZZA RICE

CONDOLEEZZA RICE

A Biography

Jacqueline Edmondson

GREENWOOD BIOGRAPHIES

GREENWOOD PRESS
WESTPORT, CONNECTICUT · LONDON

Library of Congress Cataloging-in-Publication Data

Edmondson, Jacqueline.
   Condoleezza Rice : a biography / Jacqueline Edmondson.
      p. cm. — (Greenwood biographies, ISSN 1540–4900)
   Includes bibliographical references and index.
   ISBN 0–313–33607–5
   1. Rice, Condoleezza, 1954. 2. Stateswomen—United States—Biography.
3. Women cabinet officers—United States—Biography. 4. Cabinet officers—United
States—Biography. 5. United States—Foreign relations—2001–. 6. Bush, George W.
(George Walker), 1946—Friends and associates. 7. United States. Dept. of
State—Biography. I. Title. II. Series.
E840.8.R48E26   2006
327.12730092—dc22   2006007008

British Library Cataloguing in Publication Data is available.

This book is included in the African American Experience database from Greenwood
Electronic Media. For more information, visit www.africanamericanexperience.com.

Library of Congress Catalog Card Number: 2006007008
ISBN: 0–313–33607–5
ISSN: 1540–4900

First published in 2006

Greenwood Press, 88 Post Road West, Westport, CT 06881
An imprint of Greenwood Publishing Group, Inc.
www.greenwood.com

Printed in the United States of America

The paper used in this book complies with the
Permanent Paper Standard issued by the National
Information Standards Organization (Z39.48–1984).

10   9   8   7   6   5   4   3   2   1

To Luke and Jacob
To my nephews Jonathan and Ryan

CONTENTS

Photo essay follows page 42

SERIES FOREWORD

In response to high school and public library needs, Greenwood developed this distinguished series of full-length biographies specifically for student use. Prepared by field experts and professionals, these engaging biographies are tailored for high school students who need challenging yet accessible biographies. Ideal for secondary school assignments, the length, format and subject areas are designed to meet educators' requirements and students' interests.

Greenwood offers an extensive selection of biographies spanning all curriculum related subject areas including social studies, the sciences, literature and the arts, history and politics, as well as popular culture, covering public figures and famous personalities from all time periods and backgrounds, both historic and contemporary, who have made an impact on American and/or world culture. Greenwood biographies were chosen based on comprehensive feedback from librarians and educators. Consideration was given to both curriculum relevance and inherent interest. The result is an intriguing mix of the well known and the unexpected, the saints and sinners from long-ago history and contemporary pop culture. Readers will find a wide array of subject choices from fascinating crime figures like Al Capone to inspiring pioneers like Margaret Mead, from the greatest minds of our time like Stephen Hawking to the most amazing success stories of our day like J. K. Rowling.

While the emphasis is on fact, not glorification, the books are meant to be fun to read. Each volume provides in-depth information about the subject's life from birth through childhood, the teen years, and adulthood. A thorough account relates family background and education, traces personal and professional influences, and explores struggles, accomplishments, and contributions. A timeline highlights the most significant life events against a historical perspective. Bibliographies supplement the reference value of each volume.

ACKNOWLEDGMENTS

I would like to thank Katy Poole, Kurt Vinhage, and Paul Vinhage for offering their ideas about this book. I would also like to thank Dr. Murry Nelson for many conversations about this project. Finally, I would like to thank Michael, Jacob, and Luke for their love and encouragement, as always.

There were many texts and resources that were invaluable in writing this book. While there is a complete list in the reference section, it is worth noting that biographies on Condoleezza Rice by Antonia Felix, Christin Dichtfield, and Mary Dodson Wade were particularly helpful sources about Rice's early life and family. Bob Woodward's book provided information on Condoleezza Rice's term as National Security Advisor.

Wikipedia, the on-line free encyclopedia, was a wonderful resource for dates, timelines, and definitions. Many of the definitions in the glossary were based on those offered in this resource.

Additional information came from some key Web sites, including:

The White House (www.whitehouse.gov)
Democracy Now (www.democracynow.org)
The Nation (www.thenation.com)
Common Dreams (www.commondreams.org)
The Washington Post (www.washingtonpost.com)
The New York Times (www.nytimes.com)

INTRODUCTION

I am especially indebted to those who fought and sacrificed in the civil rights movement so that I could be here today.
— Condoleezza Rice

Wednesday, January 26, 2005, was a cloudy, mild, winter day in Washington, D.C. Scattered raindrops added a chilly edge to the dreary calm that permeated the nation's capital. This day would appear to be like many other somber, midwinter days for most people bustling about the city, but for one person, at least, it was a day like no other. On this date, Condoleezza Rice, a 50-year-old African American woman from Birmingham, Alabama, was confirmed as secretary of state after grueling testimony before a Senate committee. She was the first African American woman to hold this powerful post in the U.S. government. She was only the second woman appointed to this post (after Madeleine Albright, secretary of state during the Clinton administration), and the second African American to fill this important role in the U.S. government (after Colin Powell during the first George W. Bush term in office).

Rice's eventual confirmation was no surprise, in spite of the intense scrutiny and the challenging questions she fielded from the committee. The senators had specific foreign policy concerns and they pushed hard for direct, honest answers. "Marlarkey," responded Senator Joe Biden when Rice claimed that 120,000 Iraqi soldiers had been trained by U.S.

troops (Hudson & Mohammed, 2005). He was certain the number was much lower.

The exchange between Biden and Rice was mild compared to the even more heated interaction between Rice and California's Senator Barbara Boxer. "I personally believe... that your loyalty to the mission you were given, to sell this war, overwhelmed your respect for the truth," Senator Boxer told Rice. "I have never, ever, lost respect for the truth in the service of anything," Rice responded, trying to hide her emotions (Hudson & Mohammed, 2005). Throughout this entire process, Rice never wavered. As both her critics and allies had come to expect, she remained ever-loyal to President Bush and his administration's policies.

In the end, Rice was confirmed by a vote of 85 to 13. While the margin was well in her favor, she received the most "No" votes of any secretary of state since 1825, when Henry Clay had 14 negative votes after he had been nominated by President John Quincy Adams. Clay's negative votes were partly based on the controversy surrounding the presidential election in 1824. When the election could not be decided by the electoral vote, it went before Congress. Clay, who was a senator at the time, voted for Adams and helped to sway the election to a victory for Adams. When Adams later appointed Clay as secretary of state, members of Congress cried foul, accusing them of a "corrupt bargain." With Rice's confirmation, however, there was no accusation of a corrupt bargain. Instead, there was controversy over her role in relation to the war in Iraq. Rice also had more negative votes than Henry Kissinger received after President Richard Nixon nominated him to be secretary of state during the Vietnam War. Minnesota Senator Mark Dayton explained his vote against Rice's confirmation: "I really don't like being lied to repeatedly, flagrantly, intentionally. It's wrong, it's undemocratic, it's un-American, and it's dangerous." (Fox News, January 30, 2005)

Although Rice was the first African American woman to experience this confirmation process, news images and live coverage of the Senate hearings were strangely reminiscent of the last time an articulate, well-educated African American woman sat in such a public forum before a panel of senators under intense scrutiny. Just 13 years earlier, when George H. W. Bush was president, law professor Anita Hill testified to a panel of 15 white male senators in the Clarence Thomas hearings. In spite of her allegations of sexual harassment against Thomas and the politically charged nature of the testimony, Thomas was later confirmed as an associate justice of the U.S. Supreme Court. That the politically conservative Thomas was to replace long-standing judge Thurgood Marshall was an irony not lost on Americans. Marshall spent his career advocating for the underrepresented in the United States through his work on landmark civil rights cases such as *Brown v. Board of Education*, which was passed the year Condoleezza Rice was born. The *Brown* legislation had a tremendous impact on Birmingham, Alabama, Rice's hometown and one of the most segregated cities in the nation prior to the American civil rights movement.

Anita Hill's testimony came on the heels of the Rodney King beatings in Los Angeles, and both presented a glimpse into America's racial culture, frozen in particular moments in black-and-white newspaper reports and on the television screens that flickered across the United States. Anita Hill later said that the hearings were more about her gender than her race, as if she was of no particular race during the hearings. While her testimony did not prevent Clarence Thomas from becoming a supreme court judge, she did succeed in increasing awareness about sexual harassment in the workplace.

As Rice sat poised before that Senate committee in her impeccable black suit, her large pearl necklace, and matching pearl earrings, it was difficult to predict what her legacy would be, particularly for women and people of color in the United States. There was no question that she had a front-row seat during some of the most trying and triumphant moments in U.S. history. Rice had served first as director and then senior director of Soviet and East European affairs, and as a special assistant to the president for national security affairs during the George H. W. Bush administration when the Soviet Union was dissolved and the Berlin Wall was torn down. Then she served as national security advisor to President George W. Bush during his first term in office. Rice was in Washington, D.C. on September 11, 2001, when airplanes piloted by terrorists crashed into the World Trade Center in New York City, the Pentagon in Washington D.C., and a field in rural Pennsylvania. She was a member of the inner circle of advisors to the president as he waged war in Afghanistan and Iraq. There was no doubt that she was knowledgeable about and a participant in major world events.

While she was not afraid to note her race and background to the panel of powerful white senators during her confirmation hearings, Condoleezza Rice's politics and policies in her various roles with the U.S. government and at Stanford University remained controversial and contested. Later, while serving as secretary of state, her presence in some cities in the United States and around the world sparked protests and heated exchanges. In addition to foreign policy concerns, Rice's positions in relation to women and minorities were not always viewed favorably. As provost at Stanford University, she was accused of making the climate less conducive for women and minority professors to earn tenure, and she recommended that all ethnic housing centers be placed in one building, which some students characterized as an effort to colonize them.

When Rice returned to Washington, D.C. from Stanford University to become national security advisor in 2000, questions of race, class, and gender loomed in many of the situations she faced, even though her governmental position did not deal directly with domestic policy issues. Just two years into her term as national security advisor, Senator Trent Lott celebrated former Senator Strom Thurmond's birthday by noting with admiration his involvement in the segregationist Dixiecrat Party in South Carolina. Rice issued no public statement in response to Lott's comments. Instead, it was reported that Lott considered calling on Condoleezza Rice and then-secretary of state Colin Powell to endorse him as he faced the media frenzy and public outrage that followed his statements. Later, it was disclosed that Thurmond had a daughter out of wedlock by an African American woman, further raising public ire regarding the contradictions and policies Thurmond represented.

On Dr. Martin Luther King Jr.'s birthday in January, 2003, just a few weeks after Thurmond's birthday celebration, President Bush declared that the University of Michigan law school's affirmative action program was unconstitutional. When Condoleezza Rice was asked to respond to the president's comments, she was careful to not contradict his position. There was no doubt that Rice was certainly living in the midst of a politically and racially charged arena, balancing many roles and responsibilities as she served the country. A few days after President Bush's statements about affirmative action aired on network news, Rice accompanied the president as he visited a predominantly African American church to discuss the importance of faith. During the visit, Rice blew kisses to the crowd, a gesture considered by critics to be "the most profound challenge to historical Black political behavior" (The Black Commentator, 2003).

Rice has been described as everything from the next Martin Luther King to a race traitor; her political alignments and strategies have been more scrutinized than those of perhaps any other member of the Bush administration's inner circle. Her decisions have been praised by some and condemned by others. In spite of this, her accomplishments are undeniable and her influence on history at the beginning of the twenty-first century is certain. Condoleezza Rice is a key figure to understand for anyone hoping to make sense of world events at this point in American history. This biography shares stories of her life, the controversies she has provoked, and contributions she has made.

READING THIS BIOGRAPHY

In historical context, Condoleezza Rice's life reflects many of the controversies, challenges, and successes that African Americans, women, and other marginalized groups face in American society at the beginning of the twenty-first century. As linguist James Gee has observed, "Americans tend to be very focused on the individual, and thus often miss the fact that the individual is simply the meeting point of many, sometimes conflicting, socially and historically defined discourses." (2001, p. 3) Condoleezza Rice's story, her experiences, and her contributions to our society give us a unique opportunity to consider the social and historical discourses of our times, both past and present. Rice, a descendent of slaves who rose to become one of the most powerful women in the world, represents many of the hopes, conflicts, and questions that characterize the beginning of the twenty-first century in American society.

At best, a biography should help us understand these historical and social contexts and movements that have simultaneously influenced and been composed of the people who are the subject of these projects. Each person lives in a particular time and place that is influenced by those who have gone before and those who are yet to come. For this reason, a biography should not only be a celebration of an individual; it should also attempt to understand these moments in history as they relate to other moments and other people. As writer Deborah Brintzman explains:

> The exploration of biography, however, cannot be limited to the nostalgia of the personal or the rhapsody of the unique. Attention must be given to the historical contexts of the past and the present, and to the antagonistic discourses that summon and construct what we take to be our subjective selves. We are all situated by race, class, and gender, and without an understanding of the social meanings that overdetermine how we invite and suppress differences, the complexity of biography is reduced either to the dreary essentialism that beneath the skin we are all the same, or to the insistence that difference can be overcome through sheer individual efforts. Each case depends upon the denial of history and the suppression of

subjectivity. Each orientation is in effect of a discourse that covers its own narrative tracks (2003, p. 232–233).

For this reason, while Condoleezza Rice is the central figure in this biography, it is not her story alone that is told here. Instead, her story allows the telling of many others that have intersected with Rice's across the course of American history. The time period considered in this book (1954–2005) was a time of struggle for many people in the United States and around the world. Civil rights, equal rights, the Cold War, civil wars, wars on drugs, illiteracy, and terror—all played out around the world as Rice moved into increasingly powerful and influential posts. I appreciate the humbling process of finding meaning in these stories and these times. Through this book, I may ask questions that Rice might not have asked and perhaps would never answer; however, these questions and the narrative that follows help us to raise even more questions and generate different understandings of American society as we deliberate and discuss the roles we, Rice, and other politically influential people play in relation to one another as we weave a broader narrative of our lives together.

TIMELINE: SIGNIFICANT EVENTS IN THE LIFE OF CONDOLEEZZA RICE

1954   Condoleezza Rice (Condi) was born on November 14 in Birmingham, Alabama. The U.S. Supreme Court passed *Brown v. Board of Education* that outlawed "separate but equal" treatment of children in American public schools.

1955   Civil rights activist Rosa Parks refused to give up her seat on a bus in Montgomery, Alabama; citywide boycotts of the bus system followed.

1956   The U.S. Supreme Court outlawed segregation on local bus lines.

1957   Condi began to play the piano.

1960   Freedom Riders encountered violent protests in Birmingham.

1962   The Cuban missile crisis brought the United States and the Soviet Union to the brink of war, an event that frightened Rice because she knew her parents could not protect her from this.

1963   Dr. Martin Luther King Jr. and members of the Southern Christian Leadership Conference (SCLC) organized a march for civil rights in Birmingham. Condi and her father, John, witnessed these events. Ku Klux Klan members bombed the 16th Street Baptist Church in Birmingham, killing Condi's friend Denise McNair and three other young girls. Condi visited Washington, D.C. and is reported to have claimed that she would be in the White House some day (Wade, 2003).

1964   Civil Rights Act of 1964 passed, prohibiting discrimination of all kinds based on race, color, religion, or national origin. The law

         also provides the federal government with the powers to enforce
         desegregation.

1965   Condi entered the Birmingham Southern Conservatory of Music
         to study piano, flute, and violin. Her family moved to Tuscaloosa,
         Alabama, where Condi's father worked as dean of students at
         Stillman College. Voting Rights Act passed.

1967   Extensive race riots in many U.S. cities, including Newark, New
         Jersey and Detroit, Michigan.

1968   Dr. Martin Luther King, Jr. was assassinated on April 4. Civil
         Rights Act of 1968 passed, prohibiting discrimination in the sale,
         rental, and financing of housing.

1969   The Rice family moved to Denver, Colorado when John assumed
         a position at the University of Denver. John earned his master's
         degree in education from the University of Denver.

1974   Condi graduated with a bachelor's degree in political science,
         cum laude and Phi Beta Kappa, from the University of Denver.
         Richard Nixon was impeached and later resigned from the
         presidency.

1975   Rice completed her master's degree in political science at the
         University of Notre Dame.

1977   Rice completed an internship at U.S. Department of State.

1979   Americans were taken hostage inside the U.S. embassy in
         Tehran, Iran. Rice attributed President Jimmy Carter's handling
         of the situation to her decision to switch from the Democratic to
         the Republican Party.

1981   Rice completed her Ph.D. at the Graduate School of International
         Studies at the University of Denver. She began postdoctoral
         studies at Stanford University. Ronald Reagan became president
         of the United States. Polish shipyard worker Lech Walesa, chair-
         man of the noncommunist trade union Solidarity, led a series of
         nonviolent protests in Poland.

1982   Angelena Rice (Condi's mother) earned her Master of Arts
         degree in education from the University of Denver.

1984   Condi Rice earned the Walter E. Gores Award, Stanford's highest
         teaching award. She published her first book, *The Soviet Union
         and the Czechoslovak Army 1948–1983: Uncertain Allegiance*.

1985   Mikhail Gorbachev becomes president of the Soviet Union.

1986   Rice moved to Washington, D.C. to complete a fellowship
         with the Council on Foreign Relations. In April, there was an
         explosion at the Chernobyl nuclear plant in northern Ukraine.
         In October, President Reagan and Soviet President Gorbachev

met in Iceland to discuss nuclear disarmament. Rice's second book, *The Gorbachev Era* (co-edited with Alexander Dallin), was published. Rice joined the board of directors of the Stanford Mid-Peninsula Urban Coalition, which provided vocational and academic assistance to minority students at risk of dropping out of high school.

1987   Rice served as visiting professor for a short time at the University of Michigan, Ann Arbor. Soviet leader Mikhail Gorbachev initiated perestroika; a series of economic reforms in the Soviet Union.

1988   The Soviet Union adopted the so-called Sinatra Doctrine, a policy of allowing neighboring Warsaw Pact nations to determine their own internal affairs. Eastern European nations began a string of revolutions to overthrow communism. Rice gave a speech at the U.S. ambassador's residence in Moscow. She also gave a speech to Bay Area Commonwealth Club on May 9. Both speeches conveyed her understanding of Soviet affairs.

1989   Rice served as director of Soviet and Eastern European affairs on the National Security Council under National Security Advisor Brent Scowcroft. She advised President George H. W. Bush on Soviet affairs, including the collapse of the Soviet Union. In July, John Rice married his second wife, Clara, a middle school principal.

1990   Rice served as presidential advisor when Soviet President Gorbachev and President George H. W. Bush met in Washington, D.C.

1991   Rice returned to Stanford University as associate professor. She earned an honorary doctorate from Morehouse College. She joined the boards of directors of Chevron Corporation, The Charles Schwab Corporation, the International Advisory Council of J. P. Morgan, and several other corporate, academic, and research groups.

1992   Rice earned the Dean's Award for Distinguished Teaching from the School of Humanities and Sciences at Stanford University. Rice was named Woman of the Year by the Women Legislators' Caucus in California. Anita Hill testified at the confirmation hearings for Clarence Thomas.

1993   Rice became full professor of political science and provost at Stanford University, a position she held until 1999. A terrorist bomb exploded under the World Trade Center in New York City.

1994   Rice earned an honorary doctorate from the University of Alabama.

1995   Rice published the book *Germany Unified and Europe Transformed: A Study in Statecraft* with coauthor Philip Zelikow; the book was awarded the Akira Iriye International History Award. Rice earned an honorary doctorate from the University of Notre Dame. John Rice received the National Alliance of Black School Educators' Living Legend Award, as well as an honorary doctorate from Daniel Hale University in Chicago.

1997   Rice served on a government committee to examine gender integration in the U.S. military. She was named to the American Academy of Arts and Sciences.

1998   Rice met George W. Bush when his father and mother introduced the two while they vacationed in Maine.

1999   Rice served as foreign policy advisor to George W. Bush as he campaigned for the presidency.

2000   Rice attended a week-long music camp in Montana where she played classical piano (she had at one time dreamed of becoming a concert pianist). Rice was nominated to become national security advisor to George W. Bush on December 17, 2000. Rice's father, John, died on December 24, just days after her nomination.

2001   Rice was sworn in as national security advisor to President Bush on January 22, 2001, the first woman to fill this post. In July, she met with Russian President Vladimir Putin. She was in Washington, D.C. on the morning of the September 11 attacks on the United States.

2002   Rice was awarded the National Association for the Advancement of Colored People (NAACP) President's Award for leadership in promoting the advancement of minorities through leadership or example.

2003   Rice received an honorary degree from the Mississippi College School of Law. The U.S.–Iraq war began.

2004   Rice testified in hearings before the 9/11 Commission. Rice celebrated her fiftieth birthday. Rice was nominated to become U.S. secretary of state.

2005   Rice completed first year as secretary of state. She traveled extensively throughout the world to encourage diplomacy and foster renewed relationships with allies.

Chapter 1

FROM SLAVERY TO POWER: CONDOLEEZZA RICE'S FAMILY AND COMMUNITY

I grew up in Birmingham, Alabama—the old Birmingham of Bull Connor, church bombings, and voter intimidation ... the Birmingham where Dr. King was thrown in jail for demonstrating without a permit. Yet there was another Birmingham, the city where my parents—John and Angelena Rice—and their friends built a thriving community in the midst of the most terrible segregation in the country.... My friends and I were raised to believe that we could do or become anything—that the only limits to our aspirations came from within.

—Condoleezza Rice

As she prepared her opening remarks to read to the panel on that dreary January, 2005 day during the Senate confirmation hearings, Condoleezza Rice must have sensed the profound implications her appointment as secretary of state held. Certainly she was well aware that she would be the first African American woman to hold this powerful position, and no doubt she reflected on the long road from slavery to power that her accomplishments represented in her family. Could Julia Rice, her great-grandmother, have imagined what her offspring would achieve when she illegally learned to read as a young slave girl? Could her grandfather, John Wesley Rice, have ever pictured his beautiful young granddaughter engaging in tough discussions with world leaders when he listened to her play the piano in his home in

Birmingham? Her mother and father told her she could be anything and accomplish anything, but could they have really known how seriously she took their advice?

Standing before Chairman Lugar, Senator Biden, Senator Feinstein, and other members of the confirmation committee, Rice made easy reference to her childhood home and her parents. Her voice did not crack and her eyes did not betray any emotions when she recalled her family, her heritage, and the commitment of countless people across several generations that brought her to the forefront of this international stage. Although Rice attributed success to the aspirations held by individuals, she could not deny the effects of collective work in the African American community to overcome slavery, oppression, and racial discrimination that began even before her great-grandmother's generation.

RISING UP

Condoleezza Rice is descended from white slave owners and black slaves who passed on to her a legacy of dignity, determination, and a strong belief in the value of education. Among her forebears were house slaves whose status gave them access to certain privileges, including learning to read and write (Felix, 2002). At that time, allowing slaves to learn to read and write was against the law because many people considered literacy among slaves to be dangerous. Slave owners feared that reading and writing would provide the tools for African Americans to question slavery and to revolt against the system that provided slave owners with economic and cultural capital. The Alabama Slavery Code of 1833 explicitly outlawed the teaching of reading and writing to any free Negro or slave:

> S31. Any person who shall attempt to teach any free person of color, or slave, to spell, read or write, shall, upon conviction thereof by indictment, be fined in a sum not less than two hundred fifty dollars, nor more than five hundred dollars. (Alabama Slavery Code, 2005)

Becoming literate posed great risk both to Condi's forebears and to those who taught them to read and write.

Condi's paternal great-grandparents, Julia Head Rice and John Wesley Rice, were both born into slavery but both could read and write. Part of Rice family lore is the story of Julia safely hiding her father's horses on the plantation during the Civil War (Felix, 2002), helping to preserve his wealth and property as a white plantation owner while she hoped to survive in the context of a war that would eventually free her. Julia and John married after the Civil War ended, and they raised their nine children as Methodists on a tenant farm in Greene County, Alabama.

One of Julia's and John's children was Condi's grandfather, John Wesley Rice Jr., who also raised cotton on a rented farm in Alabama. As a young man, he saved his money and enrolled as a student at Stillman College in Tuscaloosa, Alabama, 50 miles from his home. Condi has often told his story to others:

Grandaddy Rice was the son of a farmer in rural Alabama, but he recognized the importance of education. Around 1918, he decided he was going to get book-learning. And so he asked, in the language of the day, where a colored man could go to college. He was told about little Stillman College, a school about 50 miles away. So Grandaddy saved up his cotton for his tuition and he went off to Tuscaloosa.

After the first year, he ran out of cotton and he needed a way to pay for college. Praise be, as He often does, God gave him an answer. My grandfather asked how those other boys were staying in school, and he was told that they had what was called a scholarship. And they said that if he wanted to be a Presbyterian minister, then he could have one, too. Grandaddy Rice said, 'That's just what I had in mind.' And my family has been Presbyterian and college-educated ever since! (as quoted in Ditchfield, 2003, p. 16)

Dr. Charles Allen Stillman founded Stillman College in 1875 as a training school for African American male ministers. By the time John Rice Jr. entered the school, its size and academic programs had expanded considerably, yet Rice's goals to become a minister were well-aligned with the initial purposes of the college (see the Stillman College Web site at http://www.stillman.edu for more information on the school, its history, and its present programs and goals).

After graduating from Stillman College, John Rice Jr. went to Baton Rouge, Louisiana to serve as a minister. While in Baton Rouge, John married Theresa Hardnett, and their children, John Wesley III and Angela Theresa were born. Then the Presbyterian church sent John Rice Jr. to oversee a small mission in Birmingham, Alabama. This small group gradually grew into the Westminster Presbyterian Church under Rice's leadership, and it later played a pivotal role in his granddaughter Condi's early childhood.

At Westminster Presbyterian, John Rice Jr. ministered to members of his congregation by emphasizing two key components of the African American community: faith in God and education. He encouraged members of his congregation to send their children to Stillman College, but his encouragement did not end with words from the pulpit. In addition to his persuasive arguments, Rice demonstrated a deep commitment to these children and their families. In fact, at each semester's end he rode a bus from Birmingham to Tuscaloosa (since he did not have a car) to advocate for students who had unpaid tuition bills (Rustakoff, 2001). Unpaid bills would disqualify a student from final exams, preventing progress toward earning a college degree. Evelyn Glover, a student who benefited from Rice's advocacy, explained:

> I can see him even now, walking stern and erect to the president's door.... You did not see that back then—a black man at a white man's front door. And they'd let him in! And whatever he said, it worked, because I never knew a student he helped who didn't have an opportunity to take those exams, and I know our parents didn't have the money. (Rustakoff, 2001)

Eventually John Rice Jr.'s own son, Condi's father John Wesley Rice III, followed in his father's footsteps and attended Stillman College. After two years, he decided to transfer from Stillman to Johnson C. Smith University in Charlotte, North Carolina. In 1946, John Rice III graduated, but he did not stop his education at this point. He continued with his schooling and earned a Master of Divinity degree just two years later (Felix, 2002). Like his father, John Rice III continued a legacy that placed priority on earning a college degree and being well-educated.

After he finished his college education, John Rice III worked as a teacher at Fairfield Industrial School, in a suburb southwest of Birmingham. He also worked as a counselor at Ullman High School in downtown Birmingham (Felix, 2002). In both of these positions, John Rice III demonstrated a deep commitment to the young people he taught. His work with youth did not stop when school ended each day. Instead, he engaged in a variety of after-school activities to nurture the minds, bodies, and aspirations of the young people in his care. He coached after-school sports, provided tutoring for students who needed extra help with schoolwork, and organized clubs for students to learn how to play chess and ping-pong, and how to dance (Wade, 2003).

Later, when his father retired from the ministry, John Rice III assumed the responsibilities of ministering to the congregation at Westminster

Presbyterian Church. As a young girl, Condi watched as her father stood behind the pulpit on Sunday mornings and her mother played the organ for church services. Young Condi often "accompanied" her mother by sitting next to her on the organ bench (Felix, 2002). For the Rice family, life revolved around the church and its parishioners.

When he assumed the ministry on a full-time basis, John Rice III kept up his responsibilities at the high school. According to Alma Powell, wife of former Secretary of State Colin Powell, the principal at Ullman High School (who happened to be her uncle) was particularly pleased to have John Rice III at his school in Birmingham (Russakoff, 2001). Rice advocated for the young people in his community, much like his father had. He led a Boy Scout troop, helped to get Head Start programs in place in Birmingham, and he worked to help young African American people prepare for college entrance exams and to find part-time jobs (Felix, 2002). Through all his tireless advocacy for African American youth, John Rice encouraged them to be "twice as good" as their white peers so that they could change their position in the segregated South.

When he worked at the high school, John Rice III met Angelena Ray, a high school biology and music teacher on the faculty at Fairfield Industrial School. Angelena had graduated from Miles College, a private liberal arts school in Fairfield, Alabama. Angelena and John shared similar backgrounds, values, and aspirations. Both highly valued their Christian faith and both came from families that understood the legacy of slavery and how education could serve as a key to success in life. Angelena's father, Albert Roberston Ray III, was, like Julia Rice, the child of a white plantation owner and an educated African American servant (Russakoff, 2001). To Ray, education would help individuals to overcome the history of oppression that slavery inculcated into the fiber of American society.

Albert Ray's family likely influenced his deeply held beliefs about the importance of education. His mother believed strongly in the value of an education, and Ray's two sisters were among the first graduates of the nursing program at the Tuskegee Institute in Tuskegee, Alabama (see the National Park Service Web site at http://www.nps.gov/tuin/ for more historical information on the school). Based initially on a philosophy of self-help, The Tuskegee Institute (now Tuskegee University) trained teachers, nurses, masons, and vocational workers. After it was established by the state of Alabama in 1881, Booker T. Washington became the school's first leader. He served in this capacity until his death in 1915 and, under his tenure, the school grew in reputation and resources, bringing notable teachers including George Washington Carver, Robert Taylor, and David Williston to its faculty.

In spite of his success with this institution, Washington's approach to education was controversial and was criticized by those who felt his emphasis on vocational skills and training would keep African Americans in subordinate roles in the United States. Leading African American intellectuals and scholars, most notably W.E.B. DuBois, felt that social change for African Americans needed to begin differently. DuBois believed that focus should be placed on the education of a small group of elite African Americans. This so-called Talented Tenth would, in turn, help other African Americans to become intellectuals who could bring about social change in American society. While Washington emphasized self-help and individual success, DuBois advocated for social and political action on a broader scale. Many of his ideas helped to shape the civil rights protests in the 1950s and 1960s, even though he never participated directly in the protests or marches himself. Instead, DuBois renounced his U.S. citizenship and became a citizen of Ghana in the early 1960s, where he remained until his death in 1963 at age 95 (see DuBois, 1903/1989; Washington, 1901 for more information on the lives and philosophies of these African American leaders).

While it is not clear what Condi's grandfather thought of the debates about the form or purpose of education for African American people, it is clear that he instilled in his children a strong commitment to education and the strength of the individual. While Albert Ray worked in coal mines in Alabama, he and his wife Mattie raised five children in Alabama's segregated South, putting them all through college. He forbade his children to work for white people as housekeepers, which was a common practice at the time, and he encouraged them to avoid the public places where Jim Crow laws were in effect. If they were thirsty they would not go to a water fountain labeled "Blacks Only," and if they had to use a restroom they would wait until they got home. They would not eat in public places that had separate accommodations for African Americans. The Ray children were expected to conduct themselves with dignity, and to "Always remember you're a Ray!" (Felix, 2002, p. 36).

As his family grew in size, Albert Ray ran his own blacksmithing business and built homes for a living in addition to working in the mines (Felix, 2002). Mattie Ray gave piano lessons, passing on a love for music to her children and grandchildren. Both worked hard to provide for their family and both wanted their children to find success during a time that promised freedom but presented some of the most challenging social conditions imaginable in Alabama and the United States.

It was in this family, and with these values, that Angelena Ray was raised. In addition to being well-educated, Angelena was a beautiful, petite, and elegant young woman who was always well-dressed in the fashion of the times (Felix, 2002). When John Rice and Angelena married in 1954, John undoubtedly understood Angelena's hopes for their future. Together, John and Angelena shared many things in common, including their ancestry, their religion, and their commitment to education. They had much to anticipate as they began their lives together.

John and Angelena's only child, Condoleezza, was born on a Sunday morning, November 14, 1954, while John was giving a sermon at church (Ditchfield, 2003). Angelena created her daughter's name from the Italian musical phrase *con dolcezza*, which means "with sweetness." John simply called Condi his "Little Star," an endearment he used for her for the rest of his life (Felix, 2002). They both adored their young daughter and they strove to raise her by honoring the values they learned from their own families. In fact, when a neighbor suggested Angelena should have a second child, Angelena responded, "I can't take this love from Condi." (Felix, p. 47) John told one member of his congregation, "Condi doesn't belong to us. She belongs to God." (Felix, p. 47)

In spite of their deep love for Condi, John and Angelena could not protect her from the harsh realities of Jim Crow laws and segregation in the Deep South. Raising a young child in Birmingham in the 1950s and 1960s was no easy matter. There was much racial unrest and violence, and many challenging times.

BIRMINGHAM, ALABAMA: CITY OF SEGREGATION AND STRIFE

Condi Rice's early years were spent in Titusville, a middle-class African American community in Birmingham. Many of her neighbors were teachers, preachers, and shop owners, and many owned their own homes. Activities in Condi's community revolved around the church and the school. Her community was very tight-knit, and it is reported that Condi didn't see a white person until the Christmas after she was four years old, when her parents took her to meet Santa Claus (Wade, 2003). Titusville residents well understood the Jim Crow laws and the racial segregation and racial violence that were commonplace in the decades preceding Condoleezza Rice's birth. They relied on themselves and one another for support during these difficult times.

Jim Crow laws kept white and African American people separate in public places such as restaurants, restrooms, buses, and movie theaters. Even water fountains had signs that indicated which could be used by white people and which could be used by African American people.

The accommodations for African American people were always of lesser quality than those provided for white people, clearly sending a message that African Americans were second-class citizens. In addition to these laws, there were various social taboos that dictated how African American people and white people could interact. An African American man could not offer his hand to a white man or a white woman for a handshake. White drivers had the right of way at intersections. Whites would be served first at meals if African Americans and whites were eating together. African Americans could not kiss one another or show affection for one another in public. White people would address African American people by their first names but African American people had to use titles, such as Mr., Mrs., or Miss, when they spoke to a white person. These Black Codes, which were present in every southern state by 1914, eventually became translated into Jim Crow laws that governed the social behaviors in the segregated South (Felix, 2002).

According to historian Ronald L. F. Davis, the term Jim Crow is believed to have come from early minstrel shows in the 1800s. During these shows, a white man painted his face with charcoal or some other black substance and then danced and sang the lyrics of various songs, including "Jump Jim Crow." By 1890, the "Jump Jim Crow" act had become standard in minstrel shows and the term Jim Crow was solidified as a derogatory term many white people used when they talked about African Americans. Around this same time, whites began to codify various aspects of their lives to separate African Americans and whites in public spaces and to protect white privilege. This included designating Jim Crow cars on railroads that were intended for African Americans only, as well as marking separate facilities for eating, drinking, riding public buses, viewing movies, and other public events (see http://www.jimcrowhistory.org/history/creating2. htm for more information on the history of Jim Crow laws).

Laws were also enacted to further solidify African American people's subordinate status in American society, including the 1896 U.S. Supreme Court case of *Plessy v. Ferguson*. This famous case reinforced the separate but equal status that was supposed to be afforded African Americans in public spaces. The Supreme Court ruled that 14th Amendment rights of equal protection under the law applied only to the government, not to privately owned businesses, which further endorsed the right of white people to segregate restaurants, stores, pool and billiard rooms, and other public venues. Much violence against African Americans, including lynchings, became commonplace in communities throughout the United States in the years that followed. Davis (n.d.) reported that there were more than 3,700 cases of lynching between 1889 and 1930. Race riots and other violence throughout the Jim Crow era, which lasted until civil rights legislation was passed in 1964, continued as the Ku Klux Klan (KKK) and other groups attempted to enforce and maintain white supremacy while simultaneously preventing African Americans from experiencing the rights afforded to other Americans.

African Americans were faced with difficult challenges throughout the Jim Crow era as their safety was threatened and their ability to respond was thwarted. Members of the African American community questioned how they could change these conditions, particularly in the face of increasing violence and hostility. Some wanted the right to defend themselves, others hoped for more peaceful solutions, and still others feared that aggression would be the only option. After one particularly tragic summer, the so-called Red Summer of 1919, poet Claude McKay wrote the following poem, "If We Must Die":

If we must die, let it not be like hogs

Hunted and penned in an inglorious spot,

While round us bark the mad and hungry dogs,

Making their mock at our accursed lot.

If we must die, O let us nobly die,

So that our precious blood may not be shed

In vain; then even the monsters we defy

Shall be constrained to honor us though dead!

O kinsmen we must meet the common foe!

Though far outnumbered let us show us brave,

And for their thousand blows deal one deathblow!

What though before us lies the open grave?

Like men we'll face the murderous, cowardly pack,

Pressed to the wall, dying, but fighting back! (McKay, 1919)

McKay's poem reflects a view held by many who later joined the Black Freedom movement of the 1950s and 1960s; that is, African Americans should not stand idly by as their race was persecuted. Instead, they should be able to defend themselves and fight back when violence was used against them. This position was not held by all who sought equal rights for African Americans in America. Most notably, Dr. Martin Luther King Jr. advocated for peaceful, nonviolent protest to bring about social change.

Racial violence occurred in cities across the country throughout the Jim Crow era, from Detroit and Chicago to Tulsa, Oklahoma. Birmingham was not exempt from these acts of racial violence. Civil rights activist Anne Braden, who spent part of her childhood in Alabama, explained:

> Birmingham was so bad that race and union organizers were snatched off the streets and beaten nearly half to death in the 1930s, and racist police chief Bull Connor was doing his dirty work in the 40's as well, meaning that he was openly encouraging anti-black violence. Martin Luther King, Jr. once described Birmingham as the "most thoroughly segregated city in the United States." (as quoted in Ransby, 2003, p. 111)

In spite of the challenges and heavy-handed policies of racists such as Bull Connor and those like him, there were groups working against segregation and racism in Birmingham. In fact, much of the resistance to segregation and Jim Crow laws had roots in Birmingham and other cities in Alabama.

The Black Freedom movement began in earnest with the Montgomery, Alabama bus boycotts of the 1950s and continued through the civil rights era. While the NAACP worked for social change through litigation, the Black Freedom Movement, along with the SCLC which King founded in 1957, the Congress on Racial Equality (CORE), the National Urban League, and later the Student Nonviolent Coordinating Committee (SNCC)—the most militant of these civil rights organizations—were largely responsible for the organized protests, sit-ins, and marches in the 1960s (see Carson, 1989; Ogbar, 2004 for more information on these groups). Among these "big six" organizations there were clear differences that separated more moderate organizations from radical ones. Ogbar (2004) noted that as early as 1963 the more moderate groups that relied on whites for leadership and funding (including the NAACP and the Urban League) began to separate themselves from the more radical organizations (including SNCC and CORE).

Condi Rice grew up in the midst of these historic struggles for racial equality and human rights, and many important civil rights events happened right in Birmingham, including the Freedom Rides. CORE initiated these protests, sending 13 individuals on bus trips throughout the South to highlight the segregation problems with public bus transportation. One of the most violent attacks on these riders occurred in Birmingham on Mother's Day, May 14, 1960. White mobs severely beat the Freedom Riders as Birmingham's Public Safety Commissioner Bull Connor looked on. While he was aware of the riders and their pending arrival, Connor posted no police in the bus station that day, and Alabama's governor John Patterson remained unconcerned. Rather than apologize for the violence wrought against these riders in Birmingham, Connor stated, "When you go somewhere looking for trouble, you usually find it…. You just can't guarantee the safety of a fool and that's what these folks are, just fools" (as quoted in Cozzens, 1999).

When the Freedom Riders tried to continue their travel from Birmingham to New Orleans, the bus company would not provide a bus. Owners were afraid of having a bus destroyed by angry mobs, and bus drivers, who were white, feared for their lives. More students from Nashville joined the protests. National attention turned to Birmingham as U.S. Attorney General Robert Kennedy encouraged the Greyhound Bus Company to continue the journey, but the Freedom Riders did not make it farther than Montgomery. There they were greeted with more violence. Dr. Martin Luther King Jr. offered his support by holding a rally in Montgomery, but the National Guard had to be called in to ensure the safety of those gathered to hear King speak. More Freedom Riders joined the cause as the summer progressed and, while some made it to Mississippi, many of the Freedom Riders (more than 300) were arrested and spent the summer in jail. Although they were not able to finish their trip and many remained scarred for life from the beatings they received, the Freedom Riders nonetheless made a significant contribution to the civil rights movement by calling the attention of the Kennedy administration to the racial injustices in the South. At Robert Kennedy's request, the Interstate Commerce Commission outlawed segregation on public bus transportation beginning in September, 1961 (see Cozzens, 1991; Haskins, 1995 for more information on the Freedom Rides).

In 1963, Dr. Martin Luther King Jr., in conjunction with the SCLC, led peaceful marches throughout the South. One of the largest was in Birmingham. While the Rice family did not join the marches, John did take young Condi to see some of the events. The two also checked on some of John's students who had been arrested and held at the state fair grounds, the only place in the city large enough to detain the protesters (Wade, 2003). John did not want to put Condi in any immediate danger by participating in the marches. Television news cameras offered brutal images to the American public of Birmingham police officers spraying full-force fire hoses on children and protesters, along with images of dogs chasing protesters down the street. John did not want Condi to experience this but he did want her to know what was happening in their community. He recognized that history was being made, and young Condi would remember this. Years later, as secretary of state, Condi would invite former Freedom Riders and leaders in the civil rights movement to Washington, D.C. to participate in various events.

Condi's parents tried as best as they could to protect their young daughter from Jim Crow laws and the overt racism in Birmingham, much like Angelena's father tried to protect his own children from the harsh realities of segregation. To the extent possible in the tumultuous years after Condi was born, the Rices avoided potential confrontations with racism and they avoided segregated public places. As Condi's second cousin Connie Rice explained of the parents in Titusville, including the Rices, "They simply ignored, ignored the larger culture that you're second class, you're black, you don't count, you have no power" (Felix, 2002, p. 42). This was not always easy, especially when young Condi wanted to visit Kiddieland, a whites-only amusement park in Birmingham, or the segregated Alabama state fair. Even though Kiddieland opened once a year for African American children, the Rices did not take Condi to the park. Instead, they took her to Coney Island in New York where she could enjoy amusement park rides, cotton candy, and other entertainment in a context where segregation was not such a prominent concern (Felix, 2002).

There were times when segregation and overt racism could not be avoided. When this occurred, the Rices demanded to be treated as equals (Cunningham, 2005). In spite of their best efforts, the Rices could not always shield Condi from the harsh realities of the overt racism that surrounded them. One day when Condi and her mother were shopping for a new dress, a store clerk would not allow Condi to try it on in the whites-only dressing room. Instead, she wanted Condi to use a back storage closet. When Angelena insisted that Condi use a proper dressing room or she would not spend her money in the store, the clerk backed down and allowed Condi to use the dressing room (Ditchfield, 2003). During another shopping excursion, a white saleswoman scolded seven-year-old Condi when she brushed up against an expensive hat. Angelena again intervened, telling Condi to touch every hat in the store. Of course, Condi dutifully obeyed (Ditchfield, 2003). Unfortunately, these incidents, as painful as they must have been, would pale in comparison to the violent racism that would impact their community in the days and years to come.

September 15, 1963 was a day that shook people in Birmingham and people throughout the United States. White supremacist Ku Klux Klan members bombed the 16th Street Baptist Church, a predominantly African American congregation. Four young girls attending church services that Sunday morning were killed. Denise McNair, one of the victims, was Condi's friend, while another, Cynthia Wesley, lived next door to the Rice family. Condi and her family, just two miles away, heard and felt the explosion when it occurred. They were listening to her father deliver his Sunday sermon.

The city of Birmingham and the nation mourned this tragedy. Dr. Martin Luther King Jr. delivered the eulogy at the girls' funeral services. In the eulogy, he declared that "these children—unoffending, innocent and beautiful—did not die in vain." Nevertheless, it took many long years to convict the murderers for these crimes. Klansman Robert Chambliss was convicted in 1977, Thomas Blanton in 2001, and Bobby Cherry in 2002. The fourth Klansman, Herman Cash, died before he was convicted.

More bombings followed in the months after that church bombing, and the police did nothing in response. Vigilantes twice bombed the house of Arthur Shores, an attorney and friend of the Rice family, during the fall of 1963, after he moved into a predominantly white neighborhood. For decades, Shores had been the only African American attorney and defender of African American rights in Birmingham (Felix, 2002). This made him a target of much animosity as he fought city zoning codes and other injustices.

After Shores's home was bombed, the Ricees gave the family food and clothes (Felix, goto2002). The men in Condi's neighborhood, including her father John, formed a citizens' group that patrolled the neighborhood at night to help protect their families (Wade, 2003). They knew the police would be of no help to them as they faced this violence. Historian Pam King explained:

> The police would show up and tell everybody to get off the streets. They'd clear the streets and the Klan would through and throw the bombs. They weren't looking out for the safety of the citizens, they were just trying to clear the way for the Ku Klux Klan to come through and bomb. (as quoted in Felix, 2002, p. 57)

Since the police would not protect them, community members needed to take safety into their own hands.

Young Condi never forgot these tragic events. She was saddened by these events, particularly by the sight of the four small coffins after the church bombing. At the same time, she claimed that she never felt afraid or worried about her own safety. She missed many days of school because of bomb threats but she did not seem to fear personally for her life. Instead, she explained,

My parents were pretty good at giving the impression that they could
protect me from that, even if they couldn't. I remember being more
scared by the Cuban Missile Crisis, because that was something I'm
sure my parents couldn't protect me from. (Ditchfield, 2003, p. 18)

In the midst of the bombings, tragedies, and fear, Condi found solace
in the union of the African American community (Felix, 2002).

Although the Rice family moved from Birmingham just a few years
after these events unfolded, the community and the historic events that
occurred in the city were never far from Condi's heart or mind, even
when she was an adult. In her prepared statements before the Senate at
her secretary of state confirmation hearings, Rice explained:

The story of Birmingham's parents and teachers and children is a
story of the triumph of universal values over adversity. And those
values—a belief in democracy, and liberty, and the dignity of every
life, and the rights of every individual—unite Americans of all backgrounds, all faiths, and all colors. They provide us a common cause
in all times, a rallying point in difficult times, and a source of hope to
men and women across the globe who cherish freedom and work to
advance freedom's cause. And in these extraordinary times, it is the
duty of all of us—legislators, diplomats, civil servants, and citizens—to
uphold and advance the values that are the core of the American
identity, and that have lifted the lives of millions around the world.

The struggles for freedom that occurred in her hometown were influential in the civil rights efforts and in Condi's childhood experiences.

The Rices did their best to guard Condi and make sure she would
succeed in what they knew to be a world dominated by whites. Like their
parents and grandparents before them, they had faith that education was
the key to overcoming racist beliefs and practices. Because of this, they
tailored Condi's education with the goal of helping her to be successful in
a world dominated by white laws and practices. They instilled in her the
idea that John Rice taught to his parishioners and their children—that
you must be twice as good as the white people in order to succeed. John
and Angelena meticulously planned Condoleezza Rice's education, and
young Condi took seriously the idea that her achievement in school would
result in important changes in her life. The details of this education are
described in the chapter that follows.

Chapter 2

EDUCATING CONDI

My parents had a deep and abiding faith in God, they had a deep and abiding faith in family, and they fundamentally believed that education was what counted.

—Condoleezza Rice

When young Condoleezza Rice walked into the tall, two-story brick building with large glass windows to begin her formal schooling, she was continuing a family legacy wherein formal education much sought after and highly valued. The school Condi entered, the Brunetta C. Hill Elementary School in Birmingham, had a history that reflected many of the struggles, hopes, and commitments of the civil rights movement. From 1909 until1953, the year before Condi was born, the school was known as Graymont Colored School. As the U.S. Supreme Court's decision in *Brown v. Board of Education* was being enacted into law, a new school building was completed to accommodate the growing number of children attending, and Graymont was officially renamed to honor the woman who had led the school as principal for more than 21 years. The Brunetta C. Hill Elementary School was a centerpiece of the community, and the parents and teachers worked hard to ensure that the children who attended Hill had current books and experiences that would prepare them well for their future.

The Rice family was very much involved in contributing their time and resources to the school and its children. John and Angelena Rice belonged to a African American elite that found dignity through education, in spite of living in a system that was intended to crush it (Russakoff, 2001). Condi's parents well understood the importance of a good education. Both were college-educated and both believed that Condi would have to learn certain things well if she was to succeed. They carefully planned her academic, music, and athletic education, thoughtfully providing experiences both inside and outside of the public schools Condi attended.

SCHOOL DAYS

When she walked into school on that very first day, Condi was poised, articulate, and beautifully dressed. She was already well ahead of the other children her age when it came to her schoolwork. Because of Angelena's careful tutelage, Condi could read before she began school and she had studied many different academic and artistic subjects in the years before she began to formally attend school. When her teachers realized Condi's capabilities, they agreed to have her skip the first grade. While this would mean that Condi was a year younger than her classmates, it also would ensure that she would not need to spend her time reviewing material she already knew. Condi continued to work hard at her studies and she later skipped seventh grade, as well. Condi was very self-disciplined, a trait she attributed to the very controlled environment her parents created when she was a young child (Felix, 2002). She always took her schoolwork very seriously.

Since textbooks in schools for African American children were often old and outdated, John and Angelena bought new textbooks for Condoleezza's class so that the children could study up-to-date information (Wade, 2003). To be sure that Condi always had the most current and best-quality things to read, Condi's parents enrolled her in book clubs. There were always books in her house; she learned to read quickly so that she could get through the pile of assigned books that was constantly renewed in her home. Condi once explained, "I grew up in a family in which my parents put me into every book club, so I never developed the fine art of recreational reading." (Felix, 2002, p. 49)

Beyond expecting her to read a lot, John and Angelena also encouraged Condi's independent thinking by including her in family decisions. Young Condi helped to choose family dinner menus and family outings (Wade, 2003). John and Angelena never talked down to Condi as though she was a child. Instead, they treated her as an equal in conversations. John often discussed current events with Condi, and they talked about how these events related to history. Even before she went to school,

Condi would engage in conversations about newspaper stories and events. Her childhood neighbor Juliemma Smith explained:

> Condi was always interested in politics because as a little girl she used to call me and say things like, 'Did you see what Bull Connor did today?' She was just a little girl and she did that all the time. I would have to read the newspaper thoroughly because I wouldn't know what she was going to talk about. (Felix, 2002, p. 55)

What seemed unusual to her young friend was merely routine to young Condi.

Condi understood from an early age that she had to accomplish well beyond what was expected of her white peers if she was going to succeed in life. Her parents instilled in her the understanding that she had to far surpass others in her academic work if she was going to succeed, especially since she was African American. Condi later said, "You were taught that you were good enough, but you might have to be twice as good, given you're black." (Wade, 2003, p. 13)

Condi's education was influenced, in part, by the direction of her father's career. In 1965, John Rice went to work as a dean of students at Stillman College in Tuscaloosa, Alabama. The family moved from Birmingham to Tuscaloosa, about an hour north of their old neighborhood in Titusville. The Rices often spent summers traveling to different colleges where John took graduate courses (although he could not take courses at the University of Alabama because they did not admit African American students). Condi once recalled, "Other kids went on vacation to Yellowstone National Park. They took car trips to see national monuments. We stopped on college campuses. We once drove 100 miles out of our way to Columbus, so that I could see Ohio State University." (Ditchfield, 2003, p. 15)

In 1969, John completed his master's degree and took a job at the University of Denver. In his new position, John worked in the admissions office and he also taught courses, including one entitled "Black Experience in America." Through this course, John was able to invite notable speakers to meet with students, among them: Howard Robinson of the Congressional Black Caucus; Rev. Channing Phillips, the first African American man to be nominated to run for the U.S. presidency; Gordon Parks, the photographer and movie director and producer; and Fannie Lou Hamer, a civil rights activist and member of the SNCC who made a particularly strong impression on the young Condi (Felix, 2002). This was no small undertaking during the controversial and politically charged years that followed the civil rights movement, and John Rice demonstrated tremendous civic courage as he initiated and developed this program.

When Angelena and Condi moved 1,300 miles from Tuscaloosa to Denver with John, the family's life changed in many ways. The Rices initially settled in South Denver and they prepared to adjust to the vast differences they would find. In addition to differences in the racial climate of their new, integrated community, there were differences in the weather, the air, and the overall topography of the land. In Denver there could be snowfall of more than 60 inches each year and winterlike weather could extend well into the month of May. Birmingham typically has less than half an inch of annual snowfall and the average annual temperature remains largely in the 60s. The air in Birmingham is often thick with humidity and moisture, while the air in Denver is arid and dry. The highest geographic point in the state of Alabama is Cheaha Mountain, which peaks at 2,405 feet in the Talladega National Forest. By contrast, the city of Denver itself is 5,280 feet above sea level, which is why it is sometimes called the Mile-High City. The highest point in the state of Colorado is the 14,433-foot peak of Mt. Elbert. The geographical changes and the differences in experiences concerning race were constant reminders that the Rices were no longer in the Deep South.

In Denver, 13-year old Condi attended her first racially integrated school, St. Mary's Academy, a private Catholic school. St. Mary's Academy was just down the street from the University of Denver. The school was founded by the Sisters of Loretto in the mid-1800s with the explicit purpose of educating young girls whose parents moved west on the frontier during the gold rush. Over time, the school evolved to offer coeducational primary grade education and girls-only secondary education. St. Mary's Academy educates girls of all religious faiths in grades 9 through 12 through an academically rigorous program divided into the following disciplines: fine arts, language arts, language studies, mathematics, physical education, religious studies, science, and social studies (see http://www.smanet.org for more information on the school).

As expected, Condi did very well in school, balancing her academic schedule with music lessons and figure skating, a popular competitive sport in Denver. Her life was very full and extremely disciplined and focused, even during what can often be turbulent years for many teenagers. Condi's daily routine included waking at 4:30 each morning to go to the figure skating rink, and she attended classes, completed her homework, and practiced her piano lessons. Condi began to take figure skating lessons in Denver while her parents were enrolled in graduate courses at the University of Denver. Figure skating was a popular sport in Denver and she found that the years she had spent taking ballet and dance classes paid off on the figure skating rink (Felix, 2002). After the Rice family moved to Denver, Condi entered figure skating competitions, and she often did quite well.

In spite of her devotion to the sport, figure skating was not Condi's favorite athletic activity. Instead, her first and most long-lasting passion was for the game of football, and the Denver Broncos would soon become one of her favorite teams.

FOOTBALL, FOOTBALL, AND MORE FOOTBALL

When Condi was born, her father John was a football coach for young boys in Birmingham (Felix, 2002). While Condi often joked that her father had expected her to be born a boy and to become a linebacker, John did not let gender interfere with sharing his love for the game with his young daughter. He was eager to teach her all about his favorite game. As she was growing up, every Sunday afternoon Condi and her father watched football together. John Rice, always a teacher, instructed Condi about the rules of the game, the plays, the statistics, and the different teams (Cunningham, 2005). They also frequently listened to the all-white University of Alabama Crimson Tide games on the radio when Bear Bryant was the coach, even though the university and its football stadium were off-limits to African Americans at the time (Russakoff, 2005).

John and Condi would play football together in the backyard of their home, something they jokingly called The Rice Bowl (Ditchfield, 2003). They also went to see professional football games together whenever they had the opportunity. In Birmingham, the professional team that visited most often was the Cleveland Browns. Running back Jim Brown played for the team at the time and, with Paul Brown as the coach, Condi became a huge Cleveland fan. Her favorite player was quarterback Frank Ryan. She explained:

> He had a PhD in mathematics for one thing, which I thought was incredible…. But I'll also never forget the '64 Championship Game where really the Browns were, I think, overmatched by the Colts. But Ryan had one of those great, not flashy games. What I'd call a kind of Tom Brady game. (McManamon, 2004)

This time with her father began Condi's lifelong love for the sport, and she has even explained that her dream job would be to one day become the commissioner for the National Football League.

Football was a key part of Condi's life throughout her childhood and remained one of her favorite pastimes when she was an adult. Many of her social events involved football and she had friends who were professional football players. In fact, while Condi was completing her Ph.D. at the University of Denver, the Rice family often hosted Broncos players at their home for meals. Some of the regular guests included Rick Upchurch, Haven Moses, Louis Wright, Rubin Carter, and Eric Penick (Russakoff, 2005). Cornerback Louis Wright recalled getting to know Condi:

> You could tell right away this was not an 'Oh-those-uniforms-are-cute' kind of girl.... We'd rehash games afterwards and, oh yeah, she could get vicious about so-and-so getting knocked on his you-know-what and saying, 'You gotta bring on the heat,' talking like guys talk. You'd think: highly educated, prim and proper, cute little Condi. I'd never have believed it if I didn't see it with my own eyes. We knew then: This girl's tough. (as quoted in Russakoff, 2005)

The players would get Condi and her family tickets to both home and road games, and she began to date wide receiver Rick Upchurch. She was often seen sitting with the players' wives during the game and, while Condi is very private about this time of her life, there are some who claimed that she was engaged to be married to Upchurch (Cunningham, 2005).

Later, when she worked as provost at Stanford University, part of Condi's responsibilities included overseeing the football team. She was instrumental in bringing Tyrone Willingham to the university to serve as head coach of the Stanford Cardinals. At the time, Willingham was one of the few African Americans to lead a Division IA school. Willingham led the Stanford team to its first Rose Bowl appearance in 1999, with Condi cheering the team from the press box (Russakoff, 2005).

Condi has made many friends through her interests in football. She met her best friend Randy Bean, also a minister's daughter, when the two frequented Stanford football games together. While at Stanford, Condi also met assistant athletics director Gene Washington, who became the NFL director of football operations. The two grew to be good friends and often attended social events together (Russakoff, 2005). Perhaps her most famous football friend is President George W. Bush. Condi and the president frequently enjoy discussing and watching football together.

Journalist Dale Russakoff (2005) summed up Condi's involvement with the game:

Rice's long relationship with football reflects larger themes in her life—her closeness with her father, her intellectual intensity, her comfort level as a woman in a man's world and as an African American in a white world.

John Rice probably never imagined that this passion he shared with his daughter as they watched football on a small black-and-white television in Birmingham would become such a defining aspect of her life.

A MUSICAL HERITAGE

Angelena Rice played the organ and piano, just like her mother, grandmother, and great-grandmother before her. Angelena's mother was a piano teacher, and as a young girl Condi often watched and listened to her grandmother's piano students. Condi began to take lessons when she was three years old, with her grandmother as her teacher, and she could read music before she could read books (Cunningham, 2005). The first song she learned to play was "What a Friend We Have in Jesus," and she also learned "Amazing Grace" (Ditchfield, 2003).

Condi played in her first piano recital when she was just four years old. Years later, she explained to journalist Nicholas Lemann (2002):

It was a tea for the new teachers in the Birmingham public school system ... and somehow my mother persuaded these people to let me play this little Tchaikovsky knockoff. It was called 'A Doll's Funeral.' And I have a picture of me sitting there in this taffeta dress with a fuzzy tam on my head—I don't know where she got that idea. But that was the first time I played. And I played a lot. I would be asked to play at this or that function. And I did that until I was about ten. And then, all of a sudden, I wasn't the cute little kid anymore. And I wasn't asked to play very much anymore. And I got really bored with the piano and wanted to quit. It's the only time my parents ever intervened. My mother said, 'You're not old enough or good enough to make that decision. When you are old enough and good enough, then you can quit, but not now.' And I'm really glad she didn't let me quit. Because by the time I did decide I wasn't going to pursue it I was good enough to play just about anything that I wanted to, and that's why even today it's a great avocation.

Condi spent her early years enjoying a wide variety of music. She sang in the church choir with her mother as the accompanist. When she was six years old, her mother bought her a recording of the famous opera *Aida* (Ditchfield, 2003). She listened to baroque and classical music by Bach, Beethoven, Mozart, Brahms, Chopin, and other famous composers, and pianist Arthur Rubinstein was one of Condi's favorite musicians. As she grew older, she enjoyed popular music as well, including disco and classic rock (Felix, 2002).

In 1965, when the Ricees were still living in Alabama, young Condi entered the prestigious Birmingham Southern Conservatory of Music to study piano, flute, and violin. She was the first African American student at the newly integrated school (Felix, 2000), and it was here that she began to enter piano competitions. As she did in other aspects of her life, Condi showed extreme dedication and discipline as she studied the piano and prepared for various competitions and performances.

Condi continued to study music and enter competitions after the Rice family moved to Denver, and she participated in the choir and other musical activities at their new church, the Montview Boulevard Presbyterian Church, a racially and socially integrated congregation where John Rice served as an associate pastor (see http://montview.org/home.html for more information about this church). Condi particularly enjoyed the classical music traditions at Montview, and one of her favorite pieces was Beethoven's oratorio *Christ on the Mount of Olives* (Felix, 2002).

Condi's parents remained supportive of her musical ambitions after the family moved to Denver. They even gave her a Steinway grand piano as a gift (Wade, 2003). Steinway pianos, originally made in 1853 by German immigrant Henry Englehard Steinway, are known for their excellent quality and craftsmanship, and famous pianists including Vladimir Ashkenazy and Billy Joel, use the instrument exclusively. Steinway pianos are often quite expensive; it was reported that Condi's parents took out a loan to pay for the $13,000 instrument (Felix, 2002), and she later had the piano moved to California and to Washington, D.C. when she lived and worked in these areas.

The investment in the piano was one of the many ways the Ricees encouraged their talented daughter. They supported her in other ways, as well, including the moral support she would need as she entered difficult piano competitions. Their support paid off when, as a senior in high school, Condi won a prestigious piano competition in Denver. Condi played one of her favorite pieces—Mozart's *Piano Concerto in D Minor*. Mozart composed this concerto in 1785 and it is one of only two of Mozart's 27 piano concertos written in a minor key. This particular concerto was a piece Beethoven especially enjoyed, and he wrote two cadenzas for it. The concerto opens with a romantic and yet stormy and mysterious first movement, and then progresses into a more lyrical second movement called "Romanza." The concerto concludes with returns to the stormy nature of the first movement. Throughout the piece, there are intricate exchanges between the piano and the orchestra. It is a challenging and stirring concerto, one that requires great technique and musicality by the pianist. Condi successfully pulled this off, impressing judges and fellow competitors alike. As winner of the piano competition, she had the privilege of playing with the Denver Symphony Orchestra (Cunningham, 2005).

Once the competition was completed, Condi had serious decisions to make about the direction her university studies would take. She was considering continuing her studies to become a concert pianist, her dream since childhood. The next several years would require her continued discipline, talent, and ability as she focused on designing her future.

GOING TO COLLEGE

Condi has said, "In America, with education and hard work, it really does not matter where you came from; it matters only where you are going." (Wade, 2003, p. 34) While it was always clear to Condi that she would go to college, this was not as easy and the path was not always as certain as she may have initially expected, even though she was extremely successful in her schoolwork.

While at St. Mary's, Condi ran into one particularly unexpected snag as she prepared to go to college. Like most college-bound high school students, Condi took the Scholastic Achievement Test (SAT). Even though she had an excellent academic record, for some reason she did not score particularly well on the exam. When she met with her high school guidance counselor after her test scores arrived, Condi was informed that she was really not college material (Wade, 2003). Although the counselor at the school did not think that Condi should try to go to college, Condi and her family knew better. They had other plans. Later, when Condi reflected on this counselor's advice, she referred to it as a "subtle form of racism," and attributed it to a larger problem of low expectations for African American students (Ditchfield, 2003, p. 24).

Condi finished her high school requirements a year early, but she did not want to completely leave high school until her scheduled graduation. Although her parents encouraged her to enroll full-time in classes at the University of Denver, Condi compromised with them and took university classes each morning and attended classes at St. Mary's Academy each afternoon (Felix, 2002). She was just 16 years of age when she began to attend the University of Denver (see http://www.du.edu for more information about this university). As she had done her whole life, Condi maintained an ambitious schedule that would be typical for her in the years to come. She continued to start her day by taking figure skating lessons at 4:30 A.M., followed by classes, studying, piano lessons, and other activities.

Although she was a young freshman when compared with her class-mates, Condi was confident in her academic work. Ditchfield (2003) reported that during her first year in college, Condi even challenged a professor in a class in front of 250 other students. The professor presented physicist William Shockley's teachings to the class as though these were factual and true. Shockley believed that white people were genetically superior to African American people. Condi is reported to have said, "You really shouldn't be presenting these as fact, because there is plenty of evidence to the contrary." She proceeded to explain, "I'm the one who speaks French here. I'm the one who plays Beethoven. I'm better at your culture than you are! Obviously, these things can be taught. It doesn't have anything to do with whether or not you are black." (p. 25).

Condi studied piano during her first two years at the University of Denver. Although initially she considered going to a music conservatory such as Julliard, her father dissuaded her from this, hoping she would keep her educational options more broad (Felix, 2002). It seemed that this was sound advice, particularly at the end of Condi's second full year of study. Condi began to become dissatisfied with the piano performance option she was pursuing, and she wondered if this was really the right direction for her. While she was quite talented at the piano, she realized that she was not extraordinary and that it would be difficult to be successful as a concert pianist. "Mozart never had to practice," Condi noted. "I was going to have to practice and practice and practice—and still never be extraordinary." (Ditchfield, 2003, p. 26) After she finished her second year in college, Condi attended a summer music festival in Aspen, Colorado. While there, she finally concluded that, even though she was quite good on the piano, she was probably not good enough to become a concert pianist (Cunningham, 2005). Although she could have become a music teacher, she decided against it. She once said that she did not want to teach children how to "murder Beethoven," and she seemed content to keep the piano as her primary avocation.

In spite of not pursuing a professional career in music, Condi never regretted her decision. The piano continued to be a major part of her life. When she was national security advisor to President George W. Bush, she explained to Gilbert Kaplan of New York Public Radio:

I don't regret giving up the music career because I know that I was probably [with my penchant for not practicing as much as I should have and for also not having really prodigious talent] that I was probably not headed where I wanted to be in music. But the great thing about music is that you can love it all of your life, you can pick it up at different phases. (New York Public Radio, 2005)

Over the years, she played for church groups and with various chamber music groups, and when she was national security advisor during the first George W. Bush administration, she performed at Constitution Hall with the famous cellist Yo-Yo Ma. The pair performed during the ceremony to award famous Americans with National Medals of Arts and National Humanities Medals. Rice and Ma played the slow movement of Brahm's *Violin Sonata in D Minor*. At the end of the performance, the audience came to its feet, offering Rice and Ma a standing ovation.

Over the years and throughout the various phases of her life, Condi continued to play the piano several times each week. It seemed to be an important outlet for her as she assumed increasingly high-profile positions. Condi told someone who asked her whether playing the piano relaxed her, "The great thing about playing classical music is that you can't hold anything else in your head ... it's not relaxing to play Mozart of Brahms; it's challenging. But in its challenge, it takes you into another space, and I love that." (Wade, 2003, p. 32)

While Condi was certain at the end of her sophomore year in college that she should not pursue a career in music, she faced much uncertainty about what her academic pursuits should be. As she began her junior year at the University of Denver, she had not yet declared her major. She explored different courses in English, political science, and other areas (Felix, 2002). One of the classes Condi took, a course in international politics where she began to learn about different forms of government, changed the direction of her life in significant ways. Dr. Josef Korbel taught the class. One day, he lectured about Joseph Stalin and the communism of the Soviet Union. Korbel had been an ambassador in his native Czechoslovakia but he had to flee the country during World War II when the Nazis invaded. Korbel eventually made his way to the United States, where he was known to be a "fiercely loyal citizen" (Wade, 2003, p. 19). He later was head of the Department of International Relations at the University of Denver, and he was teaching in this capacity when Condi met him. Although neither of them could have predicted it at the time, Condi and Korbel's daughter Madeleine Albright would later share much in common that extended beyond their devotion to Korbel and the intellectual influence he had on their lives. Albright was the first woman to serve as U.S. secretary of state, appointed during the Bill Clinton administration, and Condi would follow in her shoes a few short years later.

After hearing Korbel's lecture on Stalin, Condi soon changed the direction of her studies. Dr. Korbel became her mentor as she pursued her bachelor's degree in international relations. Rice studied the history and politics of the Soviet Union. Her parents were supportive of her decision but admittedly were surprised at first. John Rice said, "Condi is the kind of person who is very sure of herself and makes excellent decisions ... but political science? Here's the time for fainting. Blacks didn't do political science." (Felix, 2002, p. 87)

Later Condi said that Dr. Korbel was one of the most influential figures in her life (Ditchfield, 2003). In many ways, she patterned her intellectual and academic life after him (Felix, 2002). As she completed her degree in political science, Condi studied governments, the Soviet Union, and she even learned to speak Russian fluently. The Russian language with its Cyrillic alphabet and unusual grammatical patterns can be difficult to learn, but Condi seemed to grasp the complexities readily. The Russian language gives tremendous insight to the culture and values of its people, as any language does. For example, in Russian there is no possessive form to show ownership in the same way there is in the English language. Rather than saying, "That is *my* pen," as an English speaker would, a Russian would say "By me there is a pen."

As could be expected, Condi was quite successful in her studies at the University of Denver. She was a member of Phi Beta Kappa, the honor society, and she graduated *cum laude* (with honors) from the University of Denver in 1974 with a bachelor's degree in international relations when she was just 19 years old. Condi was one of 10 students in her graduating class to win the Political Science Honors Award, which recognized students who showed outstanding accomplishment and promise in the field of political science. At her graduation ceremony, Condi was also awarded the Outstanding Senior Woman award, which the university describes as "the highest honor granted to the female member of the senior class whose personal scholarship, responsibilities, achievements and contributions to the University throughout her University career deserve recognition" (Felix, 2002, p. 98). Her distinguished accomplishments set her apart from her classmates and prepared her well for the graduate school studies that followed.

With her degree in hand, Rice headed to the University of Notre Dame in South Bend, Indiana to earn a master's degree through one of the best political science departments in the country. She liked the way Notre Dame combined religious education with its academic classes (Cunningham, 2005), and she would be able to continue to pursue her interests in studying Russian history, the Soviet Union, and the Russian language. The Department of Governmental and International Studies at Notre Dame was considered to have one of the top Soviet studies centers, led by Stephen D. Kertesz, a former Hungarian diplomat and émigré to the United States (Felix, 2002).

While at Notre Dame, Condi studied with Dr. George Brinkley, a graduate of Columbia University who was noted for his scholarship on Leninism, Kruschev, and the relationship between the Soviet Union and the United Nations. Because he recognized her talent, ability, and drive, Dr. Brinkley set up a unique program of study for Condi that included many independent study courses where she worked in a one-on-one setting with her professor. During this time, Condi became particularly interested in balance of power issues, military strategy, and Hans Morgenthau's ideas about political realism (Felix, 2002). This interest would be instrumental in the future direction of her research and her ideas about political strategy. Her culminating master's thesis focused on the Soviet military.

When she finished her master's degree in 1975, Condi initially considered going to law school. However, Dr. Korbel encouraged her to instead become a professor. Although he died in 1977 from stomach cancer, never seeing his vision for her realized, Korbel's influence remained strong throughout Condi's career and life. In 1975, the 20-year-old returned to the University of Denver to complete her doctorate. She enrolled in Denver's Graduate School of International Studies (GSIS), a program Korbel founded, and she began to work toward the completion of her Ph.D. (see http://www.du.edu/gsis/index.html for current information on this program). Her professors included Karen Feste, who completed her Ph.D. at the University of Minnesota and had prior experience with organizations in Egypt and Kuwait; Jonathan Adelman, who completed his Ph.D. at Columbia University and had worked as a visiting professor in Beijing and Moscow; and Catherine Kelleher, an expert on security issues (Felix, 2002). Dr. Adelman would serve as her dissertation adviser (see http://www.du.edu/gsis/faculty/adelman.html for more information on Dr. Adelman's research), with Dr. David Bayley, Dr. Michael Fry, and Dr. Catherine Kelleher were committee members who advised, discussed, and challenged Condi's research.

As part of her program of study, Condi had the opportunity to travel in the United States and abroad. During the summer of 1977, she completed an internship with the U.S. Department of State in Washington, D.C. While in graduate school, she also took a seven-week trip to the Soviet Union, stopping briefly in Poland en route. In Moscow and St. Petersburg, she was able to conduct research but was also able to enjoy the Russian culture and language as she walked the streets around the Kremlin, visited concert halls, and interacted with the Russian people (Felix, 2002).

Condi's dissertation research focused on comparative military regimes, and she specifically analyzed the Czech military's influence on the nation's society and politics. Condi's dissertation, entitled *The Politics of Client Command: The Case for Czechoslovakia 1948–1963*, was considered a unique contribution to the field. This work later served as the basis for her first book, *The Soviet Union and the Czechoslovak Army, 1948–1983: Uncertain Allegiance*, published by Princeton University Press in 1984.

Condi obtained her Ph.D. from the University of Denver on August 14, 1981. Members of the faculty who attended the graduation ceremony were well aware of the potential for the now-Dr. Condoleezza Rice to make an incredible contribution to the field of political science in the years to come (Felix, 2002). However, they probably could not have guessed how her contributions would come to impact the world.

MAKE HER BELIEVE SHE CAN FLY

After her graduation, Condi moved to California. She was the first woman awarded a fellowship at Stanford's Center for International Study and Arms Control. Typically, the center did not accept students from state universities such as the University of Denver (Lemann, 2002). Instead, the center sought out students from more prestigious schools such as Harvard or Yale. Condi's accomplishment in being accepted as a woman, a African American woman, and a graduate othe University of Denver was more profound than might first appear, and she had much to look forward to with this appointment.

As a member of the center, Condi embarked on more detailed studies of military arms control. While at Stanford, she made a lasting impression on the faculty. She was smart, articulate, had a gracious style, and her talent was obvious. When her fellowship was completed, she assumed a professorship at Stanford (described in more detail in the next chapter).

Condi's move to California separated her from her parents. By the time she graduated, her father had been promoted to an associate dean of the College of Arts and Sciences and he later served as the vice chancellor of university resources. John played an instrumental role in turning the

University of Denver into a African American intellectual center and in fostering an awareness of African American culture on the campus (Felix, 2002). Condi's mother earned a master's degree in education from the University of Denver in 1982. Unfortunately, she died in 1985 when she was just 61 years old, after a 15-year battle with breast cancer. After Angelena's funeral, Condi played hymns on the piano as a tribute to her mother (Cunningham, 2005).

John Rice, who married Clara Bailey after Angelena's death, lived until 2000. He watched proudly as his daughter accomplished things he never could have imagined when he sat beside her on Sunday afternoons watching football. He died just six days after she was appointed George W. Bush's national security advisor. Although he was too sick to attend her appointment ceremony, he watched her appointment on television. It is difficult to imagine the pride he must have felt at that moment.

Condi's parents certainly were key in shaping her education and experiences. Connie Rice explained, "[John and Angelena] wanted the world. They wanted [Condi] to be free of any kind of shackles, mentally or physically, and they wanted her to own the world. And to give a child that kind of entitlement, you have to love her to death and make her believe that she can fly." (Felix, 2002, p. 40)

Condi was always appreciative of her parents and the unconditional love and support they offered to her. She once said, "Every night I pray and say, 'Thank you, God, for giving me the parents you gave me.' I was so fortunate to have these extraordinary people as my parents." (Ditchfield, 2003, p. 9)

Chapter 3

ENTERING ACADEME

Condoleezza Rice's first university position when she finished her graduate program was at Stanford University in Palo Alto, California. For Rice, the Stanford campus would have been quite a contrast to her prior campus experiences. The University of Denver has a nice urban campus, while Notre Dame, with its famous Gold Dome (the Basilica of the Sacred Heart) is marked by prominent Catholic themes. Stanford's campus was and is one of the most impressive campuses in the United States. Set on more than 15,000 acres at the edge of the city of Palo Alto, it rolls right into the foothills of the Santa Cruz mountains, which are also part of campus. These foothills turn golden brown in the summer, adding to the beauty and splendor of the campus.

Rice would have entered Stanford University from the town or the railroad station on a long entrance road, Palm Drive, which is flanked by enormous palm trees on either side. Here she would have been able to see many of the campus's original buildings and quads as the Stanford family designed them. These buildings are done in the Romanesque, Italianate style that the Stanford family was familiar with from many visits to Italy. The central campus is closed to through auto traffic, so it is a beehive of bicycles, walkers and, at times, lounging students. The Mediterranean-type climate means that there is no rain from May to October (generally) and the campus greens up beautifully with the rain that falls from November to April. The beautiful Lake Lagunita is located on the campus and is the site for sailing and rowing. Many of the "wild" parts campus are rich with eucalyptus trees, which are particularly odiferous in the rainy season. The original, massive sandstone buildings with distinctive red roofs are arranged in two large quadrangles, similar to many English universities. The enormous Stanford church with its impressive frescoes dominates one quadrangle. The Hoover Institution's tower overlooks the center of campus, and visitors to the top of the tower can enjoy a spectacular view of the campus from 20 stories high. In time, Condoleezza Rice would have an office in the Hoover Memorial building, adjacent to this prominent tower. However, when she first arrived, her sense of excitement must have been tempered by some nervousness about what her future would be at this institution. This chapter details her experiences at Stanford as she climbed the ranks from a research fellow to a full professor.

UNIVERSITY LIFE

Rice began her academic career through a postdoctoral fellowship program at Stanford University's Center for International Security and Arms Control. This center was part of the university's Institute for International Studies. The goal of the institute has been to provide a forum for interdisciplinary policy research on key international issues and challenges. Members of the institute are expected to influence international policy through scholarship and analysis (see http://siis. stanford.edu/ for more information on the institute and its fellowship programs. Please note that on September 1, 2005, the institute was renamed as the Freeman Spogli Institute for International Studies at Stanford University, in recognition of the $50 million gift to the institute from the former alumnae Bradford Freeman and Ronald Spogli, who are partners in the private investment firm Freeman Spogli & Company).

Rice's fellowship paid $30,000 per year. Along with the stipend, she had an office on campus and access to all of the university's resources, including libraries, faculty, and other facilities. The fellowship supported her research on contemporary international policy issues related to the Soviet Union. This was certainly a relevant and important topic in the 1980s. Important world events were unfolding even as Rice was finding her way to Stanford. In 1981, Ronald Reagan began his first term as president of the United States, surviving an assassination attempt just 69 days into his first year in office. Entering the White House within the context of the Cold War, Reagan held strong views about the need to overthrow communism; his administration supported groups that were trying to overthrow communist regimes, including guerrillas in Afghanistan, Cambodia, Angola, and Nicaragua.

One group that came to the Reagan administration's attention that was likely of interest to Rice was the Polish group Solidarity, a national

trade union leading a nonviolent revolution in Poland through a series
of anticommunist workers' strikes. In November of 1981, then-Secretary
of State Alexander Haig sent correspondence to President Reagan about
Solidarity. By that time the group had enlisted 9 million members.
Haig noted that the success of this group, led by shipyard electrician
Lech Walesa, could confound Soviet power over Eastern Europe and
could open the way for Western values in the former Soviet Bloc. By
December 12 of the same year, in a move that surprised the U.S. government, the Polish government led by Wojciech Jaruzelski used its military
to suppress this group and established martial law throughout the country, imprisoning Walesa and many members of Solidarity. The Polish
government, as well as the Russian government, perceived this group
to be too much of a threat to let it continue. Although Walesa won
the Nobel Peace Price in 1983 for his effort to peacefully lead change
in Poland, Solidarity was forced underground throughout most of the
1980s. In spite of this, a series of nationwide strikes in the late 1980s
forced dialogue with the government, and Solidarity's successful efforts
in 1989 elections were credited with a series of peaceful anticommunist
counterrevolutions throughout Eastern and Central Europe. These were
certainly critical moments in Soviet and Eastern European history, and
Rice was well-poised to follow these events and to offer interpretations
of these policies and issues.

Shortly after Rice arrived at Stanford, she gave a talk to members of
the political science department. She impressed the faculty a great deal
and, while they did not necessarily need another specialist on Soviet
policy, they did need to diversify their faculty (Felix, 2002). As a result,
the university decided to offer Rice a three-year position on the faculty
of the political science department, where she would be the only African
American. During that time, she would need to prove herself. If she was
successful in her research, teaching, and service to the university, she
would be able to stay at the university and be eligible to earn tenure.
Tenure is an important accomplishment for a professor because it offers
both job security and a measure of academic freedom. Once a professor
has earned tenure, he or she cannot be fired from their position unless
there has been a significant professional incompetence, conviction of
a felony, or some similar misconduct. This job security allows a professor to openly pursue research areas that are of interest and is intended
to increase research productivity. These research areas may sometimes
challenge authority and question the status quo; nevertheless, a tenured
professor would not be fired for such a line of inquiry. The decision to
award a professor tenure is made after careful review of the scholar's work

by committees of the professor's peers, the university administration, and the university's board of trustees.

By all accounts, Rice was a popular professor at Stanford. She encouraged students to find their passion in their areas of study. She reassured parents, "Don't panic if your kid comes home and says, 'I'm going to major in Etruscan Art.' Who knows? Maybe they'll manage to turn that into something they can actually make a living from. You're never really fulfilled unless you find something you love to do." (Ditchfield, 2003, p. 32)

Rice taught mostly applied political science courses at Stanford. The courses she taught included Soviet Bloc and the Third World; The Role of Military in Politics; The Politics of Alliances; Political Elites; U.S. and Soviet National Security Policies: The Responsibilities of Empire in the Nuclear Age; The Institutions of Violence; and The Transformation of Europe (Felix, 2002). These classes were timely in relation to world events unfolding throughout the 1980s and 1990s. Students had opportunities to follow key world events that changed political boundaries and the course of politics around the globe. Rice's classes were popular both because of the issues considered by the students and because of her teaching style.

Rice employed different teaching strategies to engage students in her class. She often had students recreate major foreign policy decisions through role-playing exercises. In this way, she hoped students would come to understand the complexity of policy making as personality, emotion, experience, and research combined to influence individual roles and decisions (Felix, 2002). Another common teaching strategy Rice used was making football analogies as she explained political strategies. She often compared football to war, explaining that both were about taking territory. Rice was not the first to utilize such a comparison. Walter Camp, who founded the game in the early 1890s, as well as President Theodore Roosevelt and *The Red Badge of Courage* author Stephen Crane also employed this analogy (Felix, 2002).

Rice was very passionate about her teaching and was enthusiastic about the subjects she taught. She was also very open and honest about her own opinions and views on the issues she discussed in class. Students knew she was a Republican and they understood the political views she held, even if they did not share her perspectives (Felix, 2002). Her focus was on educating the students as they considered complex problems of Soviet history in relation to Eastern Europe and the world, and this often involved having them consider views that were different from their own positions on issues.

Rice's initial years at Stanford University were full, challenging, and quite successful. The year 1984 was particularly eventful and rewarding

for her, as that year she was given Stanford's highest award for teaching—
the Walter E. Gores Award. This award is given to three faculty members
each year: one tenured faculty with at least 10 years of service, one junior
faculty member, and one teaching assistant. Rice won the award as a
junior faculty member, providing wonderful affirmation of her successful work with students in the classroom. Students are often involved in
nominating faculty for such recognition, further adding to the sense of
pride a faculty member may experience when the award is announced.

In addition to that teaching award, in 1984 Rice published her first
book, *The Soviet Union and the Czechoslovak Army 1948–1983: Uncertain
Allegiance*. The book, based on her Ph.D. dissertation, is about the ways in
which the Soviet Union controlled satellite countries in Eastern Europe by
interacting with military elites in various countries. It is dedicated to her
parents and to Dr. Josef Korbel "in memory of his love for Czechoslovakia,"
and the book begins with acknowledgments of the many colleagues,
friends, and research assistants who supported her with hard work and
good humor through the arduous process of bringing the book to press.

Reviews of Rice's book tended to be positive. Mark Kramer (1985)
from Balliol College at the University of Oxford considered Rice's
research to be comprehensive, systematic, and a "model of perspicacity,
assiduous scholarship, and balanced judgment." (p. 528) Walter Ullman
(1986) of Syracuse University noted that there was no denying the
quality of the research, even if one did not agree with Rice's conclusion
that "the Czechoslovak People's Army stands suspended between the
Czechoslovak nation and the Socialist world order." (p. 245) Christopher
Jones (1986) from the University of Washington claimed the work was
a definitive study on Czechloslovak civil–military relations and that it
would have a tremendous influence on other studies of civil–military
relations in other Warsaw Pact nations.

While many found Rice's research to be groundbreaking, there were
critics, as well. Dr. Joseph Kaldova wrote a less than flattering appraisal of
Rice's work in the *American Historical Review*. Specifically, Kaldova criticized what he perceived to be Rice's inability to sift facts from propaganda
and accurate information from misinformation. He felt that as part of her
research Rice should have consulted General Jan Senja, who had access
to Warsaw Pact documents and was the highest military official to defect
from the former Soviet Bloc. Kaldova felt Rice's research, particularly her
generalizations, reflected a lack of knowledge about history and national-
ity in Czechoslovakia. For one example, Rice referred to the people of
Czechoslovakia as Czechoslovaks, while Kaldova pointed out that the
people were either Czechs or Slovaks (Kaldova, 2004).

Nevertheless, Rice's successes at Stanford and in the political science community resulted in the continuation of her position as a tenure-track assistant professor at Stanford. While she was not awarded tenure just yet, being in a tenure-track position gave her more security within the institution. It typically takes a professor six years to earn tenure and promotion to the rank of associate professor, and Rice had only been at the university for three years.

In addition to her teaching responsibilities, Rice became a fellow at the Center for International Security and Arms Control at Stanford (Ditchfield, 2003). In 1985, she also became a fellow at the Hoover Institution, a prestigious think tank founded in honor of former U.S. President Herbert Hoover. At the Hoover Institution, researchers study issues of war, revolution, and peace (see http://www-hoover.stanford.edu/ for more information on the institution, current fellows, and research reports).

During this Hoover fellowship year, Rice co-edited her second book with Dr. Alexander Dallin, *The Gorbachev Era.* Published in 1986 by the Stanford Alumni Press Service, the book provided a collection of articles and essays written by various scholars about crises and changes facing the Soviet Union and consequences these might have. The written articles were based on a lecture series supported by the alumni association, and from the time the lectures were initially offered and the book was published, the leadership of the Soviet Union had undergone dramatic changes. At the beginning of the project, Konstantin Chernenko was general secretary of the Communist party, Dmitri Ustinov was minister of defense, and Andrew Gromyko was foreign minister. When the book went to press, Chernenko and Ustinov were dead and Gromyko had been promoted to a ceremonial post in the Soviet government (Dallin and Rice, 1986, p. ix). Mikhail Gorbachev was the new general secretary for the Communist party. These dramatic changes offered a unique opportunity for Dallin and Rice to organize a timely and insightful study of the changes that were occurring.

While Dr. Dallin and Rice brought different political perspectives to the project, they were able to work together quite well (Felix, 2002). Dallin contributed three essays to the volume and his wife, Dr. Gail Lapidus, an expert on Soviet affairs from the University of California Berkely, contributed two essays. Other contributing authors included Dr. Coit Blacker and Dr. Gregory Freidin from Stanford, Dean Kendall Bailes from the University of California, Irvine, Dr. George Breslauer from the University of California, Berkeley, Dr. Timothy Colton from the University of Toronto, Dr. Robert Conquest from the Hoover

Institution, and Professor Marie Lavigne from the University of Paris. Rice contributed two essays to the volume: "The Development of Soviet Military Power" and "The Soviet Alliance System."

By 1987, Rice was promoted to associate professor with tenure, and by 1993, when she was just 38 years old, Rice was promoted to full professor. This is a young age to be promoted to such a position. The status of full professor is recognition that a scholar has made a significant contribution to the field of study and it solidifies an individual's status as a qualified expert in a particular area. The same year she earned full professorship, Rice also won a second teaching award from Stanford University, the School of Humanities and Sciences Dean's Award for Distinguished Teaching. The award included a $5,000 cash prize as well as a $1,000 increase in her annual salary (Felix, 2002).

Rice's third book, *Germany Unified and Europe Transformed: A Study in Statecraft* was coauthored with Philip Zelikow, who served in George H. W. Bush's administration during the years of German reunification. Published in 1995 by Harvard University Press, the book recounts the extraordinary diplomatic events that led to Germany's reunification in 1989 and 1990, using documents and accounts from Germany, the United States, and the Soviet Union. Both Zelikow and Rice were working for the George H. W. Bush administration during the reunification, and both brought unique perspectives to the project in light of this involvement. While reviewer Hugo Miller, of St. Edmund's College in Cambridge, UK, felt more attention could have been spent on the transformation of Europe, he praised the work for its "insidedness," for those aspects that could only be relayed by those directly participating in the events. Miller found that the book offered detailed chronicle that dispelled popular myths surrounding German reunification, particularly the notion that reunification was inevitable and therefore was relatively easy to negotiate (Miller, 1996). Reviewer Thomas Schwartz (1997) from Vanderbilt University praised the book as "remarkable," in part for its portrayal of George H. W. Bush as an accomplished diplomat in his dealings with Germany's Chancellor Helmut Kohl. Schwartz concluded that the book was a definitive account of the diplomatic success involved with German reunification. While Andrei Markovits (1996) from the University of California, Santa Cruz felt the book had no real argument and no synthesis of data, he did praise the book for what he considered its value in the detailed account of the events surrounding Germany's unification.

Germany Unified and Europe Transformed was generally well-received and earned praise from historians and scholars around the world. In addition, the book won three notable awards, the Akira Iriye International History Book Award for 1994–1995 (one of three books honored for making a significant contribution in scholarship in international history); co-winner of the 1996 Book of Distinction on American Diplomacy awarded by the American Academy of Diplomacy; and the Citation for Excellence for nonfiction foreign affairs by the Overseas Press Club of America (Felix, 2002).

Rice clearly had a strong research record. In 1999 and 2000, the *Journal of Blacks in Higher Education* listed Rice among the 40 black scholars in the United States who had the most citations of their research. This meant that other scholars were referring to her work in their writing. William Julius Wilson and Cornell West consistently topped this prestigious list, and other notable members included Toni Morrison, Lani Guinier, Derrick Bell, Patricia J. Williams, Robin D. G. Kelley, and Michael Dyson. Rice's work was clearly being noticed.

In addition to research and teaching, Rice engaged in service activities to the university and the local community. At Stanford University, she was a member and chair of various university committees, including the Public Service Steering Committee, the Committee on Undergraduate Admissions and Financial Aid, the Executive Committee of the Institute for International Studies, and the Graduate Admissions Committee. In addition, she served as the director of graduate studies and she was a member of the Faculty Council, which helps to direct university policy, in 1988 and 1989 (Felix, 2002).

Rice showed tremendous dedication to both her undergraduate and graduate student advisees. One former Ph.D. student, Jendayi Frazier, became a recognized expert on African policy. Frazier went on to teach at the University of Denver's Graduate School of International Studies and then at Harvard University's Kennedy School of Government (Felix, 2002). Later, when Rice was national security advisor, she worked on African affairs for the National Security Council. When Rice became secretary of state, Frazier became the assistant secretary of state for African affairs and the top advisor to the President on foreign policy issues in Africa. In these roles, Frazier faced criticism that her loyalty to Bush promoted her own career but seriously compromised the lives and well-being of people in Africa (WBAI, 2004).

Dr. Josef Korbel's encouragement to Rice to enter academe and become a professor was certainly prescient and sound advice. By all accounts, Rice was successful in her work as a professor, advancing through the ranks to full professor by relying on the discipline and focused hard work that her parents had taught her from a young age. Rice's future as an academic at

Stanford University seemed to be promising, but requests from Stanford administrators and Washington, D.C. forced her to make some difficult choices. Before turning to these decisions, however, we will consider some of the other aspects of Rice's life during these early years of her academic life at Stanford.

IN HER FREE TIME

In spite of her busy schedule and extensive responsibilities at the university, Rice had quite a full life outside of her academic work. She was involved in the local community and she continued to spend focused time on music and football. Through these various activities, she found time to spend with friends.

Like her parents, she showed a tremendous commitment to the young people in her community; she began various initiatives to help youth to be successful in school and to prepare for college. One such initiative was in 1986, when Rice joined a group that helped to train minority students for work and college (Cunningham, 2005). A second initiative for young people involved her father John and his second wife, Clara: In 1990s, Rice cofounded the Center for a New Generation, an educational support fund for schools in East Palo Alto and East Menlo Park in California. The program served children in grades three through eight who attended the school where Clara served as principal. This was an after-school program to offer education in language, performing arts, computers, math, and science for promising young students. Stanford University students volunteered to help teach the children enrolled in the center, and noted dignitaries, including Colin Powell, sometimes visited (Cunningham, 2005). Rice, who also served as vice president of the Boys and Girls Club of the Peninsula, often relied on her own growing-up experiences as she worked with the center. "The idea is that if you give kids in underprivileged circumstances hands-on support in math, science, language arts, and music, then they'll have every reason to achieve. I was given that as a child, and I try very hard to pass that on." (Rice, as quoted in Ditchfield, 2003, p. 99)

While at Stanford, Rice also found time to continue her involvement with music, always an important part of her life. She even played the piano for church services for six months when a church was in need of an organist. Occasionally, Rice gave concerts on the Stanford campus, and she was sometimes heard practicing or offering impromptu performances. One such performance happened in the St. Anthony Hotel in San Antonio, Texas in 1998. Rice practiced a Brahms piece in the hotel lobby before the Stanford Cardinal basketball team played in the Final Four match at the Alamodome, the first time the team had played in the semifinal match since 1942. "I've got a concert at Dink next week," Rice explained. "I'm desperate. This may be the only time I have to practice" (as quoted in Acosta, 1998). She referred to Dinkelspiel Auditorium, one of the major entertainment venues on the Stanford campus.

In her free time, Rice continued to watch football and she had season tickets to Stanford ball games. She sometimes traveled to out-of-town games to cheer for the team and many of her social relationships evolved around the game. While in Stanford, she had a few romantic relationships, including one with San Francisco 49ers wide receiver Gene Washington (Felix, 2002). Washington, who was a Birmingham native and Stanford alumnus, played with the 49ers between 1969 and 1977. He also had various cameo roles in films and television, and later became the director of National Football League (NFL) operations.

Rice enjoyed cooking, particularly Southern cuisine, seafood gumbo, and fried chicken. She also enjoyed getting together with friends and shopping, one of her favorite pastimes. Rice had a penchant for fashionable shoes, and she would often shop at San Francisco's famous Union Square with her childhood friend Deborah Carson to buy Ferragamos and other topline brands (Felix, 2002). Once, she purchased eight pairs by the Italian designer in one shopping excursion alone. Union Square has always been an exclusive place to shop. Along with luxury boutiques and lavish department stores, there are other cultural and arts exhibits and galleries to explore in the hilly streets of the city that surround the square.

Continuing the routines she began as a young person, Rice always made time for exercising. She often rose as early as 5:00 A.M., to lift weights, run on a treadmill, or engage in some other physical activity with headphones blaring her favorite Led Zeppelin tunes. At Stanford she had personal trainers from the athletic department who helped her with strength training and other workout routines (Felix, 2002).

FIRST-HAND EXPERIENCES WITH POLICY

As a professor at Stanford, Rice had several opportunities to gain first-hand experience with the workings of foreign policy. The first came in 1984, when one of her colleagues, Coit Blacker, introduced her to Gary Hart, a senator from Colorado who ran for president in 1984 and 1988. Rice offered Hart some foreign policy advice for a short time, something she no doubt remembered when, years later (prior to the September 11 attacks), Hart offered her advice on foreign policy and potential terrorist attacks (a point discussed in more detail in Chapter 4). Rice's advice to Hart was never borne out in a presidential administration, however. Although Hart was a Democratic front-runner in the 1988 campaign, a scandal involving his extramarital relationship with former model Donna Rice forced him to withdraw from the race.

During her professorship, Rice also offered important service in Washington. In 1986 she was awarded one of 20 fellowships offered to academics to spend a year as a fellow with the Council on Foreign Relations. There she studied and reported on America's relationship with other countries, particularly communist nations (Cunningham, 2005). Rice's former professor from Notre Dame, Dr. George Brinkley, nominated her for the fellowship program. The council, which was founded in 1921, holds annual meetings, disseminates information through its journal *Foreign Affairs*, and recruits a range of scholars and analysts to study and publish information through its web site and other forums about foreign policy issues. People as varied as W.E.B. DuBois and Henry Kissinger have published in the council's journal or other publication venues (see http://www.cfr.org/index.php for more information on the council).

Although Rice was unaware of it at the time, her year as a fellow with the Council on Foreign Relations was just a small taste of what would become her future in Washington. Her time in Washington in 1986 gave her insight into the workings of the Pentagon, the military, and the Reagan administration's dealings with the Soviet Union, particularly around issues of nuclear weapons. Even though President Reagan stated that he dreamed of a world free of nuclear weapons, the arms race was deadlier than ever at the end of his first term in office. The Strategic Defense Initiative, commonly referred to as Star Wars, was a priority to Reagan. He planned to use space-based systems to protect the United States from a nuclear attack, even though critics pointed out problems with this plan. Rice would have been aware of the issues and plans of this adminstration, as well as the tension around these issues between Secretary of State George Schultz's office and the National Security Council (see Evans, 1998 for more detail).

In 1986, Mikhail Gorbachev was the new leader of the Soviet Union. He became general secretary of the Communist party in March, 1985, after his predecessor Konstantin Chernenko died. Chernenko's leadership of the Soviet Union was noted for escalating Cold War tensions between the United States and the Soviet Union and a return to the more hard-line Soviet policies that characterized the Breshnev era. Gorbachev brought a markedly different leadership to the Soviet Union.

At 54 years of age, he was the first Soviet leader born after the 1917 Russian revolution. He never knew what it was to live in a country ruled by tsars; his only experience with his homeland was as a communist state. Gorbachev began his administration with hopes to change relations between the Soviet Union and the Western world, particularly the United States.

On October 16, 1986, Gorbachev met with President Ronald Reagan in Reykjavik, Iceland to discuss changes in the intermediate-range nuclear weapons in Europe. This was the beginning of many dramatic changes to come in the next years, which were dubbed Gorbachev's Sinatra Doctrine. This doctrine loosened Soviet restrictions on the internal affairs of Warsaw Pact countries, including Czechoslovakia, Poland, Bulgaria, Romania, Hungary, and East Germany. The Sinatra Doctrine, which was jokingly labeled as such in reference to Frank Sinatra's song "My Way," led to a string of revolutions in Eastern Europe through 1989. As each country went its "own way," communism peacefully collapsed (with the exception of the violent overthrow of the communist regime in Romania) and the Cold War ended.

Rice was poised to witness and analyze these historical changes. Her time in Washington in 1986 was a brief prelude to a longer period in the nation's capital, a dream she harbored from her childhood.

A young Condoleezza with a confident smile. Courtesy of University of Denver Special Collections and Archives.

Condoleezza Rice was always stylish and well-dressed. Courtesy of University of Denver Special Collections and Archives.

Condoleezza Rice in July of 1974. At 19 years of age, she finished her undergraduate degree at the University of Denver and was making plans to attend graduate school at Notre Dame. Courtesy of University of Denver Special Collections and Archives.

In 1990, Dr. Condoleezza Rice served the George H.W. Bush administration. Courtesy of University of Denver Special Collections and Archives.

Condoleezza Rice in 1999, ready to serve as adviser to George W. Bush. Courtesy of University of Denver Special Collections and Archives.

Condoleezza Rice, as Secretary of State, met with many foreign dignitaries including NATO Secretary Jaap de Hoop Scheffer. Courtesy of NATO Photos.

In 2005, Rice became the first African American woman to serve as Secretary of State. Courtesy of the U.S. State Department.

Chapter 4

DR. RICE GOES TO WASHINGTON

When Condoleezza Rice was 10 years old, she visited Washington, D.C. with her parents. It was a long drive from Birmingham to the nation's capital, made longer by the fact that the Rice family had to sleep in the car. There were no hotels that would allow African American people to stay in a room, and so they had no other choice (Ditchfield, 2003). When they arrived in the city, the Rices went to Pennsylvania Avenue and stood on the sidewalk in front of the White House. As she gazed at the stately building where presidents and dignitaries lived and worked, young Condi said, "One day I will be in that house." (Wade, 2003) And of course, one day she was.

Her affiliations with power in Washington began in 1985 when Rice attended a talk given by Brent Scowcroft at Stanford University. She asked tough questions and exuded a confident manner that greatly impressed Scowcroft. He later recalled, "Here was this young slip of a girl who would speak up unabashedly." (Ratnesar, 1999) After the talk, Scowcroft got to know Rice better and he invited her to join some foreign policy sessions at the Aspen Institute (Prados, 2004). At the time, Scowcroft was codirector of the Aspen Strategy Group (see http://www.aspeninstitute.org for more information). Here Rice would eventually join company with Dick Cheney, Donald Rumsfeld, Philip Zelikow, Paul Wolfowitz, and other government officials who would be her colleagues over many years to come as they worked for the George H. W. Bush and George W. Bush administrations.

After her year of service on the Council of Foreign Relations ended in 1986, Rice returned to Stanford University to resume her duties as an associate professor. She had plenty of work to do, and she certainly had gained new insights on her research given her year of experience in Washington. Her ideas, opinions, and expertise were much in demand.

Upon her return to Stanford, Rice gave a series of speeches that reached broad audiences throughout the country, raising her profile among academics and policymakers. In 1987, Rice was invited to the University of Michigan at Ann Arbor to be a visiting scholar. During her brief visit to the university, she offered a public lecture on Mikhail Gorbachev and led a seminar for students at the Center for Russian and East European Studies (Felix, 2002). With her book *The Gorbachev Era* published the year before, she no doubt had much to share with the students in Ann Arbor that would be of interest to them.

In the spring of 1988, Rice made a trip to the Soviet Union to give a speech at the U.S. ambassador's residence in Moscow (Felix, 2002). Her speech was the inaugural talk in a series of speeches at the ambassador's home. While in Moscow, she spoke about arms control policy and an upcoming summit with the United States. Writers for *The Moscow Times* seemed surprised that a young African American woman could give such a well-informed talk about Soviet policy:

> The men ...couldn't help wondering: "She should be busy cooking and driving her admirers mad. But instead she aptly juggles numbers of missiles and tanks, names of marshals and dates of summits." (as quoted in Associated Press, 2000)

Rice was just 34 years old at the time she delivered her speech in this prestigious international venue.

Rice's visit to Moscow was followed by a high-profile speech on May 9, 1988 the Commonwealth Club in San Francisco. The Commonwealth Club is considered the nation's oldest and largest public affairs forum, with over 16,000 members and 400 annual events. The club considers politics, culture, the economy, and society in its various lecture series (see http://www.commonwealthclub.org for more information on current events). Founded in 1903, the club's impressive speech series has included Teddy Roosevelt, Erin Brokovich, Bill Clinton, Desmond Tutu, Cesar Chavez, Lech Walesa, and other notable dignitaries from the United States and abroad. The club's weekly radio broadcast began in 1924 and is considered the oldest in the nation. Rice's speech, which was broadcast live on the radio throughout the country, was entitled "U.S.–Soviet Relations: The Gorbachev Era."

While Rice seemed to be pleased to be back in California, her time at Stanford would be short-lived. Brent Scowcroft remembered Rice from their meeting in 1985, and he likely paid close attention to her accomplishments over the years after their initial conversations. In 1989, Scowcroft became national security advisor during the George H. W. Bush administration. Shortly after Bush won the election, Rice received a telephone call from the Scowcroft asking her to join his team as a Soviet analyst. Rice was about to move back to Washington for a more extended period of work at the White House.

THE GEORGE H. W. BUSH ADMINISTRATION: THE FORTY-FIRST PRESIDENT

After accepting Scowcroft's offer, Rice took over as the director of Soviet and Eastern European affairs within the National Security Council, reporting to the president on Soviet affairs. She was probably thrilled to be working with someone as experienced as Scowcroft. Before serving as national security advisor, Brent Scowcroft had worked for the federal government in a variety of capacities. He had been a lieutenant general in the U.S. Air Force and he had extensive experience in Washington. He also served as a military assistant to President Richard Nixon and was national security advisor to President Gerald Ford before serving the George H. W. Bush administration in the same capacity.

Rice and Scowcroft seemed to have much in common. In addition to their shared interest in the Soviet Union, Soviet history, and the Russian language, Felix (2002) noted that both held a commitment to so-called power politics, an international relations policy in which powerful countries threaten to use particular economic or political strategies, including war, to protect their own sovereignty in the world. Nuclear arms development, covert operations, and tariffs are just some of the ways in which countries work to protect their own power (see Roy, 2001 for one discussion of the problems with this form of politics). The philosophy Rice and Scowcroft shared would allow them to work seamlessly together.

Scowcroft would become a longstanding mentor to Rice. He guided her through her first years in the National Security Council and he remained a close mentor when she later became George W. Bush's national security advisor. Scowcroft's influence was readily apparent, so much so that when she was advisor to George W. Bush during his 2000 presidential campaign, writer David Plotz (2000) would observe that Rice was "Brent Scowcroft in the body of a African American woman."

As a member of Scowcroft's national security team, Rice became quickly noted as indispensable to the president, particularly as major historical events unfolded in Eastern Europe and the Soviet Union. Rice was quickly thrust into the world arena as a series of events in the late 1980s resulted in the fall of the Berlin Wall. This brought a significant change to the geographic, political, military, and social relations and conditions throughout Eastern Europe. When Rice assumed her responsibilities with the National Security Council, the Berlin Wall, erected in 1961 as a 28-mile, barbed-wire fence between post-World War II East and West Berlin, was a fortified structure with concrete walls, guarded by troops, that physically encircled the city of West Berlin. Over the years, scores of people attempted to cross the barrier; nearly 200 lost their lives. The wall served as a symbol of the Cold War between communism and the Western world. When she joined the National Security Council, Rice supported the idea that Germany should be reunited, a position some in the Bush administration felt was risky (Cunningham, 2005); she also felt that securing the reunification of Germany was the key to ending the Cold War. In spite of her position on this, Rice likely did not anticipate that she would see this reunification realized while she was serving in the George H. W. Bush administration.

A series of events led to the fall of the Berlin Wall and Germany's eventual reunification. In addition to unrest in Poland, on August 23, 1989, Hungary ceased its border restrictions with Austria, and East Germans began to escape through Hungary. There were mass demonstrations by East Germans against their government. In the fall of that year, East German Mayor Erich Honecker resigned and Egon Krenz assumed temporary responsibilities as mayor. Krenz decided to allow temporary travel visas to West Berlin, but Propaganda Minister Gunter Schabowski misreported information about this to the press. On November 9, 1989, during a press conference, he read a note that said East Berliners could travel to West Berlin; when word was released, thousands of East Germans went to the wall to demand entry to West Berlin. Guards, confused by the information presented to them and unable to restrain the massive crowds that gathered, began to let citizens pass freely through the wall for the first time since 1961. East and West Berliners joined in celebration at the wall, which was subsequently torn down by the jubilant crowds. Less than a year later, Germany reunited.

Shortly after the Berlin Wall came down, on December 3, 1989 President Bush traveled with Condoleezza Rice to meet with Mikhail Gorbachev on a Russian ship, the *Maxim Gorky*, anchored on Marsaxlokk Bay just off the coast of Malta. This meeting was considered by many historians to be the official end of the Cold War, although President Bush and Condoleezza Rice later pointed out that this was just one of a series of events that brought the end of the Cold War.

Before the meetings were initiated, Rice and members of the administration were concerned about having a summit with Gorbachev too early after the fall of the Berlin Wall. Although Gorbachev indicated during a speech to the United Nations in 1988 that he was allowing Eastern Europe to move in its own direction, in addition to reducing the number of Soviet troops, members of the Bush administration were primarily focused on the troop reduction. As a result, the administration did not immediately recognize the change in policy in Eastern Europe as a sign that changes were imminent. Some analysts have criticized Rice because the dissolution of the Soviet Union was an event that she seemed to not anticipate, even though these were key areas of her responsibilities in the White House. In fact, Prados (2004) noted that the Soviet retreat had been signaled before Bush took office. He wrote:

> [T]he Soviet leader announced unilateral reductions in Russia's armed forces and withdrawals from East Germany, along with what amounted to the abandonment of the Brezhnev [D]octrine (a policy that promised direct intervention should any East European nation seek to break away). The question for the United States was how best to respond. Years later, Rice admitted that by focusing exclusively on the Soviet troop reductions, "I missed completely, really, the revocation of the Brezhnev [D]octrine."

Prados continued his critique by noting that the administration ordered a pause in Soviet–American diplomacy in February 1989 that eventually became a freeze for many months. Prados claimed that Rice's failure to focus on this critical change was a significant oversight, and he felt that the same "curious inattention" would be evident again after Rice became national security advisor.

The changes that were underway placed international pressures on the Bush administration about the proper role for the United States in relation to Eastern Europe and the Soviet Union and, as Rice explained, the administration hoped to find some middle ground. Because they did not want a major summit where the administration might feel pressured into particular agreements, they turned to Malta instead (National Security Archive, 1997). To Bush administration officials, Malta seemed like a strategic place for a quiet meeting between Bush and Gorbachev. It was out of the public eye. Some in the administration, however, were concerned about the weather conditions. As it turned out, this was no small matter. Later, Rice explained:

> So we arrived in Malta. It was beautiful; everything was going just fine. And then the next day we woke up to this horrible storm. That made it very difficult to get back and forth, and a lot of the plans had to be scrapped. The notion of having one meeting on the *Belnap*, the American destroyer, and then a meeting on a Soviet ship, the *Maxim Gorky*, had to be scrapped. And since the *Maxim Gorky* was actually in port, we met all the time on the *Maxim Gorky*. But those little logistical details aside, and the fact that I don't swim very well and was terrified being in those launches trying to get out to the ships, the meetings themselves were very successful. (National Security Archive, 1997)

While on the ship, Bush immediately laid out his agenda to Gorbachev. Both leaders understood that they were working in a context where situations were rapidly changing, and administration officials felt it was crucial for Bush to indicate his support for Gorbachev's reforms that were already underway through perestroika (which literally means reconstruction and refers to a period of economic reforms Soviet leader Mikhail Gorbachev introduced in 1987). Bush wanted Gorbachev to know that there were plans for U.S.–Soviet relations, arms control, and even student exchange programs.

In addition to the significant diplomatic work that occurred at these meetings, Rice must have felt some sense of accomplishment as she came face-to-face with Mikhail Gorbachev. It was while she was on board the *Maxim Gorky* that Rice first met Gorbachev, who was so central to her research and public speeches. She described her initial encounter with him:

> I first met [Gorbachev] on this trip, and he walked up to me on the *Maxim Gorky*. President Bush was stuck out on the *Belnap*, so we were all just sort of wandering on the *Maxim Gorky*; and he walked up and I introduced myself, and I was struck right away by the fact that he seemed supremely confident, he said something about hoping that the waters of international relations weren't as rough as the waters in which we were sitting. (National Security Archive, 1997)

Later, while visiting with Gorbachev, President Bush reportedly introduced Condoleezza Rice to Gorbachev by saying, "This is Condoleezza

Rice. She tells me everything I know about the Soviet Union." To this, Gorbachev was said to reply, "I hope you know a lot." (Ratnesar, 1999)

Although the administration had been given mixed reports about Gorbachev's general attitudes before the meeting, Rice noted that Gorbachev was really quite calm and collected as the talks between Bush and Gorbachev unfolded. After Gorbachev heard Bush's plans, Rice noted that he expressed confidence that the administration was truly supportive of the changes underway in Eastern Europe and the Soviet states. Even more important to the administration, on the second day of meetings Gorbachev also indicated that he hoped the United States would remain a strong presence in Europe.

Several years later, Rice drew conclusions about the significance of these meetings:

> The Malta summit's greatest achievement, I think, was to establish a working relationship between the United States and the Soviet Union, first and foremost at the level of head of state, but also foreign ministers and the people below them. It was more getting the instruments right than any single achievement. I think we also learned a lot about Gorbachev at that time: we learned that he was not a man who was easily rattled; we learned also that he was a man who didn't particularly like to say 'No,' and I think we believed, from that time on, that if we could avoid facing him with black and white choices, a lot could happen naturally without the Soviet veto. (National Security Archive, 1997)

Furthermore, she did not believe that Malta was the end of the Cold War, as many reported. Instead, she reflected:

> I do not think that one can think of Malta as the end of the Cold War, because Germany was still divided; there were still countries in Eastern Europe that were communist; the Soviet Union was still dominant in Europe from the point of view of its military power; they were still very active in the Third World. So I would not cite Malta as the end of the Cold War, but it certainly gave us instruments that became very important as we moved toward the end of the Cold War. (National Security Archive, 1997)

Shortly after these historic events, the Soviet Union was politically dissolved. Poland, with Lech Walesa leading the Solidarity group, had already broken away from communism, as had Hungary. Romania was to follow, although the transition was marked with violence and public executions. Finally, Germany reunified, an announcement made in February, 1990, after Bush and German Chancellor Helmut Kohl met at Camp David. Rice explained:

> And the thing to understand about the Kohl announcement is that it was really an agreement between Bush and Kohl that came out of the meeting. I don't think that the Germans came to Camp David in February 1990 expecting to say a unified Germany would be in NATO. What happened was that during the discussion, President Bush said to Chancellor Kohl, "We have to have an affirmation of German intentions to be a part of NATO." And President Bush was someone who could be incredibly persuasive one on one. He himself often said he wasn't the best speech-maker in a large audience, but he had no parallel, and probably has no parallel, in one-to-one negotiations with another head of state, and he convinced Helmut Kohl that this had to be done. And at the press conference, Helmut Kohl, in answer to a question, said: [Y]es, Germany would be unified in NATO, fully into its military institutions. And he was challenged on that by a member of the German press, and he stuck to his guns. And that was another, very important turning point for us in German unification. (GWU, 2005)

This was considered a tremendous diplomatic accomplishment for the Bush administration, and one of the greatest moments of American statecraft in the history of the United States (Joffe, 1996). Bush carefully aligned himself with Germany's Chancellor Helmut Kohl as he supported far-reaching changes through Gorbachev's perestroika. These were difficult diplomatic waters to navigate, and Bush was not always in agreement with his Secretary of State James Baker or with Brent Scowcroft. However, his diplomatic abilities seemed to pay off as a peaceful end to a divided Germany was achieved and the Soviet Union loosened its grip on Eastern Europe. Rice attended the September 12, 1990 signing of the historic Treaty on the Final Settlement with Respect to Germany that occurred in Moscow. Later, Rice and her colleague Philip Zelikow would retell these events in their highly acclaimed book *Germany Reunified and Europe Transformed: A Study in Statecraft* (Zelikow & Rice, 1995).

As the Bush administration focused on Eastern Europe and Mikhail Gorbachev, yet another key figure was demanding their attention by the late 1980s. Boris Yeltsin, who was a member of the Communist Party of the Soviet Union from 1961 until July of 1990, was an outspoken critic of Gorbachev, in part because he thought reform under Gorbachev's leadership was moving too slowly. Known for his brusque manner and strong will, Yeltsin rose from his roots in a peasant family in the Sverdlovsk region of the Soviet Union to eventually lead Russia in the years after the Soviet Union was disbanded.

Yeltsin's rise to power was no easy matter. In 1989, Yeltsin became a member of the newly established Congress of People's Deputies, and he gained a seat on the Supreme Soviet. The Congress of People's Deputies, formerly known as the Congress of Soviets, had 2,250 deputies, with a smaller subset, the Supreme Soviet, coming from this group. The Supreme Soviet served as the legislature for the Soviet Union. The Congress met twice each year, while the Supreme Soviet met during the entire year. The Supreme Soviet would make decisions about all but the very most important issues, which the Congress would determine.

When Boris Yeltsin visited Washington in 1989, members of the Bush administration were cautious in their approach. They were dealing with Mikhail Gorbachev and hoping to maintain smooth relationships with the Soviet Union. Rather than having a meeting with President Bush, administration officials instead planned for Yeltsin to meet with National Security Advisor Brent Scowcroft. When Yeltsin realized this plan, he was not pleased and insisted on meeting with President Bush, even though he didn't have a meeting scheduled. Yeltsin became even more angry when he thought he was being admitted through a side door into the White House. He didn't realize that the front door is only used for formal state events. Condoleezza Rice was sent to greet Yeltsin and to assuage his concerns. She recognized that he was accustomed to being in charge and, using her perfect Russian, Rice firmly told Yeltsin that his meeting was with Scowcroft and not with President Bush, although Bush did stop by the meeting to greet Yeltsin and speak with him for a few minutes. Rice described the encounter and her general impressions of Yeltsin:

> [Yeltsin] stood in the basement of the White House and told me that he would not go until I guaranteed him that he was going to meet with President Bush. We're not accustomed to that kind of attitude in the White House, but it is part of his strength. He is capable of mobilizing himself that way. But I think therein lies his weakness too. I would agree completely with what has been said. This is the man who is best in crisis. But once the crisis over, he has a tendency to withdraw from the stage. He has a tendency to be

unable or uninterested in the day to day problems of governance. (NewsHour, July 4, 1996)

Rice was able to calm Yeltsin and lead him to his meeting with Scowcroft.

By 1990, Yeltsin's status in Russia was increasing. He was the speaker for the Supreme Soviet of the Russian Soviet Federated Socialist Republic, which would later become known as Russia after the Soviet Union collapsed. By this time, he was known for his harsh criticisms of Gorbachev, and he called for Gorbachev to be harsher with conservatives and to give more power to the republics. In June, 1990, Yeltsin quit the Communist party and on June 12, 1991, he won 57 percent of the vote to defeat Nikolai Ryzhkov to be elected as Russia's first president. After a coup against Gorbachev on August 18,1991, which detained Gorbachev in the Crimea, Yeltsin went to Moscow to defy the insurgency. Yeltsin led mass opposition to the coup, delivering a memorable speech from the top of Military Tank No. 110 of the Taman Division of the Red Army. Yeltsin declared that the coup was unconstitutional and he demanded Gorbachev's release. After this, the coup leaders left Moscow, Gorbachev left the Crimea, and Yeltsin was praised by leaders from around the world for the way he rallied the masses.

Gorbachev and Bush came together again in 1991 but, after the coup, Gorbachev's power was severely compromised. By November, 1991, Yeltsin banned the Communist party in Russia, and in December, 1991, the Ukraine sought independence from the Soviet Union. On December 8, 1991, Yeltsin met with Ukrainian President Leonid Kravchuk and Stanislau Shushkevich, chairman of the Supreme Soviet of Belarus. The three leaders agreed to dissolve the Soviet Union and to form the Commonwealth of Independent States (CIS).

In all, Rice served two years in Scowcroft's National Security Council during the George H. W. Bush administration. She witnessed the fall of the Iron Curtain, the end of the Cold War, and the reorganization of much of Eastern Europe and the former Soviet states. Throughout this time, Rice was widely admired by her colleagues for her pragmatism and her gentle, yet tough disposition. While in Washington, she made important connections with the Bush family and prominent lawmakers and politicians. It was during this time she became a close colleague of Philip Zelikow, who was in charge of European security affairs in Brent Scowcroft's National Security Council. Not only did the two coauthor a book based on their experiences in the Council, they would also meet again when Zelikow directed the Aspen Strategy Group. However, with the entry of Bill Clinton, a Democrat, to the White House in 1992, Rice faced yet another change. She packed her bags and headed back to California to rejoin her colleagues at Stanford University.

RETURN TO STANFORD

Although Brent Scowcroft asked Rice to continue on the National Security Council when her first term of service ended, she declined the invitation. It was time to return to her teaching. While she was grateful for the opportunity to participate in the historical events that unfolded during her time in Washington, and while she greatly admired President Bush, Condoleezza Rice returned to Stanford University and resumed her duties as professor in 1991. On May 1, 1991, she gave a speech at Stanford as part of a two-day symposium on "The New Soviet Union." In her speech, Rice recounted her experiences as an advisor to the president. She explained two key challenges she perceived with the new Russia: First, the United States would need to figure out how to respond to Russia in matters of foreign diplomacy, and second, the United States would need to determine how to help the Russia with its own economic reform. She felt this would be particularly challenging since the states of the former Soviet Union had no monetary system, no banking system, and no clear sense of how to reform their economy. She explained the challenges the administration faced as the power struggles between Yeltsin and Gorbachev were evident, and the discouragement she experienced when Soviet Foreign Minister Edvard Shevardnadze resigned in 1991. Overall, however, she concluded that the former Soviet Union had come a long way and that life would be better for the Russian people in the years to come (Stanford University News Service, 1991).

As she returned to teaching, meeting with graduate students, and serving on university committees, Rice seemed happy with her work. She explained:

It's terrific to be back.... People have been universally welcoming and warm.... Two years is about as long as one could be away and keep an academic career on track. I could have done it for several more years, but I had such a ride, I don't feel any lack of completion in what I did. (Stanford University News Service, 1991)

She described her work with President Bush, whom she met with personally up to three times a day before the Malta summit, and she characterized the President as "a first-class diplomat." (Stanford University News Service, 1991)

Rice seemed to be glad to be back at the university. Her office hours in Washington were typically from 7:15 A.M. to 8:30 or 9 P.M. each day, and her travel pace was quite hectic. Between March and September, 1990, she traveled to Germany 10 times (Stanford University News Service, 1991). At the university, she would have more control over her time and her agenda. She explained:

> [An academic setting is] one of the few places where people pay you to do what you want to do. In government, your schedule is never your own. I was completely driven by other people and events—I could never plan a day. But that was more than compensated by the sheer energy and ether of the job. (Stanford University News Service, 1991)

Rice would no longer be busy meeting with the president. Instead, she would be busy catching up with her graduate students, two of whom were close to finishing their dissertations. She would also prepare for yet another trip to Russia and for courses that she would be teaching in comparative politics, the role of the military in Russian politics, and transitions in Europe over the next year.

After returning to Stanford in 1991, Rice accepted an appointment from California Governor Pete Wilson to serve on the committee to reorganize California's legislative and congressional districts. While some felt Rice should run for public office, she declined, even though many thought she should seek the seat in the California senate that Wilson vacated when he became California's governor (Ditchfield, 2003). Instead, Rice seemed to be refocused on her work with the university and committed to her research and teaching.

On December 13, 1991, Rice returned to the prestigious Commonwealth Club to deliver another speech broadcast live on the radio. In this speech, "End of the Cold War: Challenges for U.S. Policy," she discussed the economic and political challenges facing Russia and she shared some of her own insider perspectives on these events (Felix, 2002).

However, Washington was probably never far from Rice's thoughts. She briefly returned to Washington at the start of the Clinton administration to serve as a consultant to Clinton on Russian affairs. Her close friend at the time, Strobe Talbott, had suggested to Clinton that Rice be appointed U.S. ambassador to Moscow. When word reached Stanford that Rice made a special effort to charm President Clinton, her colleagues at the conservative Hoover Institution were not particularly impressed (Lemann, 2002). Members of the institute wondered about her loyalty, particularly since she had only become a member of the Republican Party in the 1980s after she first arrived at Stanford.

On a personal level, it had made sense for Rice to become a Republican. After all, this was her father's political affiliation. Rice was well aware that in the 1950s her father was not able to register to vote with the Democratic Party in Alabama. During that time, the Dixiecrat Party had a stronghold in the state and they tried to keep African Americans from voting. African American voters were required to take difficult tests that were impossible to pass, but white voters were not. Some of the questions on the test included items such as "Who was Thomas Jefferson's great-grandmother?" or "How many windows are in the courthouse?" John Rice was also shown a jar of jellybeans and asked how many were in it. If he answered incorrectly, he could not vote (Ditchfield, 2003). The Republican Party secretly registered African American voters and they were willing to register John Rice. For this reason, he remained a Republican for his entire life.

In spite of her father's experiences, when Condoleezza Rice voted for the first time in a presidential election, she was registered in the Democratic Party and she cast her vote for Jimmy Carter. However, Rice reported that she was disappointed with Carter's knowledge and understanding of the Soviet Union and the threat it posed during the Cold War (Ditchfield, 2003). She also did not believe he handled the 1979 Iran hostage crisis particularly well.

Although she was a registered Democrat in 1980, Rice voted for Ronald Reagan for president. She supported his strong stance against communism and his support for having a powerful military (Ditchfield, 2003). Then, in 1984, Rice heard presidential candidate Walter Mondale offer a speech to the Democratic National Convention. Mondale's speech repeatedly mentioned the need to help women, minorities, and the poor. Rice did not think that women or African Americans needed to be protected or pitied, and so she finally decided to leave the Democratic Party (Ditchfield, 2003). She explained to the Republican National Convention in 2000:

I joined the party for different reasons. I found a party that sees me as an individual, not as part of a group. I found a party that puts family first. I found a party that has love of liberty at its core, and I found a party that believes that peace begins with strength. (Washington Post, 2000)

Rice clearly believed individuals could overcome societal issues. She seemed to be part of the group of middle-class African Americans that Dr. Martin Luther King Jr. criticized when he wrote in his *Letter From a Birmingham Jail* (1963)—the "few middle-class Negroes who, because of a degree of academic and economic security and because in some ways they profit by segregation, have become insensitive to the problems of the masses." Her position prompted criticisms of Rice from prominent African American intellectuals, including Patricia Williams and Michael Eric Dyson, as well as the father of Denise McNair, the young girl killed in the 16th Street Baptist Church bombing in Birmingham in 1963, who praised Rice but explained that he was unable to support her politics (Tilove, 2005).

In spite of her claims of support for the Republicans, the so-called true-blue Republicans at the Hoover Institute were uncertain about Rice because of her relative newness to the party, particularly those foreign policy experts at the Hoover Institute who had been part of the Reagan administration. Since Rice served as an informal advisor to the Gary Hart presidential campaign, which sought to defeat Reagan, they mistrusted her. However, Rice held her course, and friends noticed that she was more conservative in thought when she returned to Stanford after serving on the National Security Council (Lemann, 2002).

During the 1990s, Rice's position toward Russia began to diverge from that of other American Sovietologists (Mann, 2004). She became sharply critical of the Clinton administration's Russia policies, claiming that the administration focused too much on Yeltsin and not enough on economic reform. Rice felt that the United States should begin to detach itself from Russia's top political leaders and she thought there needed to be much tougher action to encourage Russia to stop its campaign against Chechnya. This surprised many of her colleagues. Stanford scholar Michael McFaul claimed that he was "totally shocked" by Rice's position, and others felt that Rice was really proposing a new policy of containment toward Russia. In retrospect, some have argued that she was really positioning herself politically for the upcoming Republican presidential campaign in 2000 (Mann, 2004).

Before this unfolded, however, Rice took on new responsibilities and challenges at Stanford. In 1992, Rice served on a search committee for the new Stanford University president. Gerhard Casper was hired, and in 1993 Casper asked Rice to become provost at Stanford, a position second only to the president of the university. Apparently Rice made quite an impression on the president as the interview process unfolded, and he decided she would be well-suited for this position in his administration

(Lemann, 2002). The provost is the chief academic and budget officer at the university, whose primary responsibility is to manage the school's finances. Rice was just 38 years old and the first woman and first African American to hold this prestigious post. *Time* magazine included Rice on their "50 Young Leaders to Watch" list (Cunningham, 2005), while the *Journal of Blacks in Higher Education* (1995) noted Rice's appointment on their list of milestones for African American Higher Education.

Some people at Stanford had doubts about the appointment, however. Some thought Rice had no experience for this new position and that it had been given to her primarily because of her race. Typically, a person would spend years working their way from a professorship into a position such as a provost, often first serving as a department head and a dean. Rice had done neither but, nevertheless, she was asked to assume this powerful position. In spite of speculation voiced by others, Rice never felt someone should be given a job because of race or gender. Instead, she stated, "I've always felt you should not see race and gender in everything. You should give people the benefit of the doubt." (Wade, 2003, p. 27) As provost, Rice was strongly opposed to identity politics:

> During her bravura six-year tenure as Stanford provost, her aversion to identity politics at times unsettled some faculty and students. Once, when an African-American student complained that Rice was inattentive to campus minorities, she shot back. "You don't have the standing to question my commitment," she said. "I've been black all my life." (Ratnesar, 1999)

Instead, Rice continued to hold fast to the lesson her father taught her—that she needed to be twice as good.

After she became provost, Rice served on the boards of many corporations, charities, research organizations, and the National Endowment for the Humanities (Wade, 2003). Some of the various companies and organizations she served included Transamerica, Charles Schwab, Chevron, The International Advisory Council of J. P. Morgan, the University of Notre Dame, the San Francisco Symphony, the Carnegie Corporation, the RAND foundation, the Hewlett-Packard Corporation, and the Hewlett Foundation.

The board memberships considerably supplemented Rice's university salary. For instance, after she became a board member in 1991, Chevron paid her a $35,000 per year retainer, $1,500 for each meeting she attended, and shares in the company that were worth $241,000 by her 10th year (Felix, 2002). As a Chevron board member she also worked on an oil pipeline project in Kazakhstan, which was one of the United States's largest overseas energy investments (Felix, 2002). In 1993, Chevron named an oil tanker the *U.S.S. Condoleezza Rice* in her honor; Rice traveled to Rio de Janeiro to christen the vessel. Her 10-year service to Chevron was perhaps among the more controversial of her board work. A group of Stanford students who opposed Rice being invited to speak at the 2002 Stanford graduation listed some of their concerns about her work with the Chevron board because of the company's environmental degradation and human rights abuses in Nigeria and in Richmond, California (Redwood Action Team at Stanford, 2002; Appendix 2). By 2001, the tanker was quietly renamed the *Altair Voyager* after discussions with Rice's National Security Council office. It was a reminder of the George W. Bush administration's ties to the oil industry, and officials wished to diminish the visibility of this connection and concerns about conflicts of interest (Marinucci, 2001).

When she became Stanford provost, Rice had to make some unpopular decisions. The university was $43 million in debt and Rice had to balance the budget. An earthquake in 1989 damaged more than 200 buildings on campus and the school's expenses for health care and other items had risen over the past several years. Rice made cuts in spending and programs and she had to fire some people, including a popular Hispanic administrator. Many university faculty were unhappy because they were not involved in the decisions about these matters. Rice was known for working on her own rather than working through committees of faculty members who could help and advise her about the decisions she needed to make. Students staged sit-ins and hunger strikes in opposition to Rice. Among their complaints were the following:

- They claimed that Rice repeatedly denied tenure to women and minority faculty members, exacerbating the lack of diversity at Stanford. When she left her position as provost, only 14 percent of the faculty was female, significantly lower than the 25 percent national average.
- They claimed that Rice defended Stanford's hiring and tenure processes in spite of formal complaints from 15 female professors who documented discriminatory practices. Rice's controversial statistical data was used to defend the university's practices.
- They claimed that Rice weakened the popular Student Workshops on Political and Social Issues program because of a lack of funds.

- They faulted Rice for locating all the ethnic community centers in one building (Old Union), making it a "people of color" colony on the campus. The African American Student Union resisted this relocation, and Rice placed this group in a dilapidated building that had a defective roof.
- Rice reportedly denied departmental status to the African American Studies program and other ethnic studies programs. Instead, she supported a Comparative Studies on Race and Ethnicity (CSRE) department that would deny departmental status for individual ethnic studies.
- Rice overturned a 1969 ruling at Stanford that had ended the Reserve Officer Training Corps (ROTC) use of Stanford facilities. Under Rice's tenure, ROTC could return to campus and offer credits for classes.
- Rice failed to work to satisfy demands of student hunger strikers.

(See Redwsood Action Team at Stanford, 2002 for further details and links to supporting documents.)

The once-popular professor now found herself in some very difficult positions. In addition to this list of complaints, there were housing shortages on campus for graduate students and difficult decisions about faculty tenure that needed to be made (Felix, 2002). Many students and faculty members did not agree with what Rice was doing, and they voiced their concerns. At the same time, there were others who still respected her leadership and courage, and the Stanford administration clearly was pleased with her work.

Rice was successfully meeting one of her primary charges as provost. She was able to turn the university's finances around and, during the six years she served as provost, Stanford met its budget. By the time of her 1996 meeting with the Faculty Senate at Stanford, she was able to report that the university was no longer running a deficit, and instead held a $14.5 million reserve. She later claimed that this was one of accomplishments she was most proud of as she looked back on her years as provost.

In 1997, Rice served on a federal government committee to examine gender-integrated training in the U.S. military. Defense Secretary William Cohen appointed Rice as one of the team of 11 civilians, and the group met with hundreds of military personnel across the country. The committee offered many recommendations to the government to improve drill sergeant training, recruitment policies, and basic training, and they offered ideas about how to expand sexual harassment instruction, provide separate barracks for men and women, and hire more women trainers (Felix, 2002).

That same year, she was nominated to the American Academy of Arts and Sciences, which awards members who have made distinguished contributions to science, scholarship, public affairs, and the arts (see http://www.amacad.org for more information). This recognition came on the heels of Rice being awarded several honorary doctorates, including one from Morehouse College in 1991, the University of Alabama in 1994, and the University of Notre Dame in 1995. Her prominence in academia was clear.

While her professional life was quite full during her years as provost, Rice continued to play classical piano. She studied further by taking private piano lessons with George Barth, an associate professor at Stanford. Rice participated in a variety of chamber music groups with faculty and deans at the university, which was an enjoyable change from her more typical solo performances. Chamber music places different demands on musicians as they learn to balance tempo and volume across complex musical scores. One highlight for Rice was when she performed Brahms's Piano Quintet in F Minor with the world-famous Muir String Quartet when they visited Stanford. To prepare, Rice had to work 10 hours each week with Barth, which took an incredible commitment (Felix, 2002). Rice also performed during faculty talent shows, including one performance with Barth. The two played Brahms's two-piano version of Variations on a Theme by Haydn. Later, she continued her contact with the Muir String Quartet and attended some of their summer institutes to continue to improve her performance skills.

In addition to her continued work on the piano, Rice challenged herself physically in the workout room. She worked with several different trainers on strength training and other aspects of her workout routine. Rice spent some time with Karen Branick, who had been Tiger Woods's strength coach when he was a student at Stanford (Felix, 2002).

By 1999, times were about to change for Rice yet again. She decided to take a one-year leave of absence from the university to explore her options in the private sector. When Rice resigned her position at Stanford, many people were disappointed, including the university's president Gerhard Casper. When she left, Casper commented on the ease with which the two had communicated, in spite of what might appear to be cultural differences (Casper was from Hamburg, Germany). He complimented her on her love of learning and presented her with a first-edition Russian language copy of *War and Peace*, printed in 1868. It was a rare and very special gift, one that Rice clearly treasured (Ditchfield, 2003). Inside the book, Caspar wrote:

> To Condoleezza Rice, May War be the fiction, and Peace the reality. With the greatest appreciation and deep gratitude for her service as Stanford's 9th Provost. (Felix, 2002, p. 221)

Chapter 5

JOINING GEORGE W. BUSH'S WHITE HOUSE

Condoleezza Rice first met George W. Bush in 1998, when the former President George H. W. Bush and his wife Barbara introduced Condi to their son while they were vacationing in Kennebunkport, Maine. President Bush believed that his eldest son would be a world leader and he wanted Rice to offer counsel to him in matters of world affairs. He once wrote about Rice to a journalist:

> Condi was brilliant, but she never tried to flaunt it while in meetings with foreign leaders … her temperament was such that she had an amazing way of getting along with people, of making a strong point without being disagreeable to those who differed …. She has a manner and presence that disarms the biggest of the big shots. Why? Because they know she knows what she is talking about. (as quoted in Felix, 2002, p. 175)

Between talks about foreign policy, George W. and Rice played tennis and went out on Bush's boat, which she allowed even though she does not like to be on the water. Rice later described their meeting:

> I don't get seasick, but I also don't like the water very much and I most certainly don't fish…. I let President and Governor Bush fish and I sat and talked. We talked a lot about the state of the American armed forces and ballistic missile defense.

She found Governor Bush to have an edgier style than his father:

> Governor Bush is somewhat more interactive. He tends to press the speaker to answer questions almost in a kind of rapid-fire manner. (Rice, as quoted in Kettmann, 2000)

When George W. Bush gave a fundraising speech for the Republican Party in San Francisco, former Secretary of State George Schultz invited the Texas governor to Stanford. Bush met with Schultz and a group of experts from the Hoover Institute. Rice attended this meeting, and she impressed the governor yet again. Soon after this, experts from Hoover began to make regular trips to Austin, Texas to hold sessions with Bush, who by then had decided to run for the U.S. presidency (Lemann, 2002).

Around this time, Rice resigned her position as provost at Stanford. Rice agreed to advise Bush on foreign affairs, and she and Paul Wolfowitz quickly assembled a team that included Richard Perle, Richard Armitage, Dov Zakheim, Stephen Hadley, Robert Blackwill, and Robert Zoellick to help with the work. The group named themselves The Vulcans, after the Roman god of fire and metallurgy, as well as a statue in Birmingham that commemorated its steel-making history (Grossman & Long, 2001). The Vulcans were a formidable group, one that even Al Gore's advisors conceded was a strong one (Plotz, 2000).

To begin her tutelage of the Texas governor, Rice made Bush a list of foreign leaders that he reviewed each day. The two shared information on foreign affairs as they exercised together on a treadmill, and Rice devoted her time to helping the future president prepare for his work with foreign leaders and policy. She no doubt drew extensively on her experiences from the first Bush administration as well as her research on Soviet and Eastern European policy during and after the Cold War.

Early in their work together, Rice found that she admired Bush's intelligence, directness, and discipline (Ditchfield, 2003). She also respected his relationship with his family. Rice once noted:

> I tremendously admire his relationship with his wife, Laura. It's beautiful, so tender and supportive. And I love his relationship with his daughters, because I had a great relationship with my father and there's nothing like that! (Ditchfield, 2003, p. 71)

Rice and Bush shared other things in common in addition to politics and exercise. Both enjoyed football and they had similar religious convictions. They quickly became close friends, and Rice spent a great deal of time with George and Laura Bush. Since Rice was essentially alone after her mother and father died, the Bushes had become like her own family (Woodward, 2002).

Throughout the 2000 presidential campaign, Rice drove home her message that a Republican president should define the national interest with key priorities:

> […]building a military ready to ensure American power, coping with rogue regimes, and managing Beijing and Moscow. Above all, the next president must be comfortable with America's special role as the world's leader. (Rice, 2000)

The campaign trail can be brutal but Rice was consistent in her message to the future president about foreign policy. She spoke of his commitment to free trade, his understandings of the benefits of the North American Free Trade Agreement (NAFTA) that came from his role as a "border governor" in Texas, and his commitment to a strong national defense (Kettmann, 2000). She spoke only rarely of terrorism or threats from Iraq. In fact, in an article she published in *Foreign Affairs*, she described what would be the new Bush administration's foreign policy (at least, initially). In the article, she focused on China and Russia and noted that Iraq and North Korea could be deterred from using weapons of mass destruction (Rice, 2000). Her position at this time was well-aligned with those of Brent Scowcroft and other political realists whose ideas were prominent throughout the Cold War (Mann, 2004).

As Bush's campaign for the presidency drew to a close, Rice found herself thrust into the national spotlight in ways she had never before experienced. On the second day of the GOP convention, August 1, 2000, on prime-time television broadcast around the world, Rice addressed the Republican National Convention in Philadelphia. After acknowledging the contributions of former Republican Presidents Gerald Ford, Ronald Reagan, and George H. W. Bush, she stated:

> And tonight, we gather to acknowledge this remarkable truth: The future belongs to liberty, fueled by markets in trade, protected by the rule of law and propelled by the fundamental rights of the individual. Information and knowledge can no longer be bottled up by the state. Prosperity flows to those who can tap the genius of their people. We have, ladies and gentlemen, a presidential nominee who knows what America must do to fulfill the promise of

this new century. We have a nominee who knows the power of truth and honor. We have a nominee…. We have a nominee who will be the next great president of the United States of America, Texas Governor George W. Bush. (Washington Post, 2000)

She finished her speech to the sound of thundering applause and to broad speculation that she was well-poised to be the next national security advisor.

Election night, November 7, 2000, did not turn out the way either candidate or campaign team expected. As the election coverage continued on network television into the wee hours of the morning, it was still not clear whether Al Gore or George W. Bush had won; in fact, it would not be clear for weeks who would be the next U.S. president. Ballots needed to be recounted, which turned out to be no small matter. Since the state of Florida used paper punch cards for ballots, it was sometimes difficult to know what voters intended when there was a "hanging chad," an incompletely punched hole that still had paper attached at two or three corners of the hold indicating a vote for a particular candidate. As the recounting of ballots began in Florida, Rice and other top administration advisors met with Bush in the governor's mansion in Texas. She appeared at his side as he spoke with the press outside the governor's mansion.

On December 13, 2000, Al Gore conceded the election after more than a month of ballot recounts, court appeals, protests, and bitter legal battles. George W. Bush was named the forty-third president of the United States. This was only the second time in U.S. history that a father and son would both serve as U.S. president. The first was John Adams, who was the second U.S. president, and his son John Quincy Adams, who was the sixth U.S. president (see Appendix 1 for a list of members of George W. Bush's Cabinet).

Just four days later, Bush appointed Rice as national security advisor. She was the first woman to hold this position. "I'm honored to have the chance," Rice said. "It's a remarkable thing. We're only what—140 years out of slavery?" (Ditchfield, 2003, p. 74). Bush said, "Dr. Rice is not only a brilliant person; she is an experienced person. She is a good manager. I trust her judgment. American will find that she is a wise person." Then he turned to her and added, "I'm so honored that you're joining this administration." (p. 75)

Rice was to serve the president and the country alongside powerful and experienced men including Dick Cheney, Donald Rumsfeld, John Ashcroft, and General Colin Powell. Since many of the members of the president's inner circle had served during President George H. W. Bush's administration, they knew Rice from her work with Brent Scowcroft and they respected her knowledge of the Russian military and government. In addition to these professional relationships, there were personal connections, as well. Colin Powell's wife, Alma, had been raised in Birmingham and she knew the Rice family. Rice spent a great deal of time with the Powells, and Colin Powell told the media that Rice was like a daughter to him. He explained, "Condi was raised first and foremost to be a lady…. She was raised … to be a person of great self-confidence in Birmingham, where there was no reason to have self-confidence because you were a tenth-class citizen and you were black." (Ditchfield, 2003, p. 76)

Rice's new duties began in earnest before the president's term officially began. One week before the inauguration, she attended a meeting at Blair House, the residence across the street from the White House where President Truman and his family lived when the White House was being renovated between 1948 and 1952. No doubt while Rice attended meetings in Blair House that day; she remembered that she once named Harry Truman her "man of the century." She said of Truman:

> [He] somehow made sense of what America's role in the world ought to be under the most difficult of circumstances, when it would have been easy for the United States to withdraw…. I look to the people of that era in amazement and wonderment at what they were able to do. (Rice, as quoted in Kettman, 2000)

Rice could hardly have anticipated at the time how she would contribute to understandings of America's role in the difficult times that were to come, some of which were previewed in the meetings at Blair House.

President-elect Bush and Vice President-elect Cheney also attended the meetings. CIA Director George Tenet and his Deputy Director of Operations James Pavitt led the briefing. They explained the top three security threats they felt were important for the new administration to know about. Osama bin Laden and his Al-Qaeda network headed the list. Tenet also cited the increasing availability of weapons of mass destruction and the rise of China's power as imminent concerns for the nation (Woodward, 2002). Rice would discover how prescient this warning would prove to be as she assumed her new responsibilities at the White House.

NATIONAL SECURITY ADVISOR

On January 30, 2001 at 3:35 P.M., George W. Bush convened the first meeting of the principals of the National Security Council. The meeting was held in the Situation Room, downstairs from the Oval Office in the West Wing of the White House. Vice President Dick Cheney, Treasury Secretary Paul O'Neill, CIA Director George Tenet, Secretary of State Colin Powell, Secretary of Defense Donald Rumsfeld, and Joint Chiefs of Staff Chairman General Hugh Shelton joined the president and Condoleezza Rice at the table. Also present at the meeting was Andy Card, White House chief of staff, and seated behind each principal was the top deputy for each respective office. At the meeting, the president made it clear what Rice's role would be. He told those in attendance, "Condi will run these meetings. I'll be seeing all of you regularly, but I want you to debate things out here and then Condi will report to me. She's my National Security Advisor" (Suskind, 2004, p. 70). The topic for the first meeting was Mideast policy, and the discussion focused initially on the Arab–Israeli conflict. Then Rice turned the group's focus toward Iraq and the ways in which that country was seen to be destabilizing the region. Rice's work was clearly underway.

As national security advisor, Rice was clearly the closest to Bush (Mann, 2004). She was the first person to meet with the president each morning, and she gave him updates on world news and events. She often helped him weigh decisions when his Defense and State departments were divided on certain issues. Her role was primarily that of manager and advisor. Rice explained: "As an advisor to the president, my job is to faithfully represent the views of different agencies that make up the National Security Council and to organize the decision-making process so that the president can come to a conclusion about what he thinks." (Ditchfield, 2003, p. 79)

The National Security Council was first formed in 1947 under the National Security Act. The act established the council, along with provisions for a secretary of defense, the Central Intelligence Agency, the National Military Establishment, and the National Security Resources Board. Initially, the secretary of state and the secretary of defense were key members of the council, along with the secretaries of the Army, Navy, Air Force, and Marines, and the chairman of the National Security Resource Board. Each council has been charged with foreign policy and defense policy coordination, but each council has looked and functioned differently depending on the needs and management style of the president. Over time, the council grew to serve the president alone as it managed competing points of view among various departments in the administration.

Under President George W. Bush, the council included the vice president, the secretary of state, the secretary of the treasury, the secretary of defense, and the assistant to the president for national security affairs. The chairman of the Joint Chiefs of Staff was the statutory military advisor to the council, and the director of Central Intelligence was the intelligence advisor. The chief of staff to the president, counsel to the president, and the assistant to the president for economic policy were invited to attend any NSC meeting. The attorney general and the director of the Office of Management and Budget were invited to attend meetings pertaining to their responsibilities. The heads of other executive departments and agencies, as well as other senior officials, were invited to attend meetings of the NSC when appropriate (see http://www. whitehouse.gov/nsc/history.html#summary for more information on the history of the National Security Council).

Rice engaged her responsibilities as national security advisor a bit differently than did her mentor, Brent Scowcroft. In addition to eventually diverging from Scowcroft's tradition of political realism, which emphasized tough policies to support national interest and balance of power diplomacy (Mann, 2004), she had a different public persona. Where Scowcroft and many other national security advisors remained largely out of the public eye, Rice was seen frequently on television news programs and in public forums offering explanations of the administration's priorities and policies. Some in the media compared Rice's visibility to that of Henry Kissinger of the Nixon administration and Sandy Berger of the Clinton administration. In her new role, Rice traveled a great deal with the president, meeting with heads of state of different countries around the world. Rice frequently explained the president's position to the media during press conferences. In the very early days of the administration, this often involved explaining the president's stance on the Kyoto Protocol and the environment. In turn, the media paid a great deal of attention to Rice. In the year 2000, she had more than 3,800 citations in the national press, 10 times more than she had in 1999 (Journal of Blacks in Higher Education, 2001). Rice even appeared on the cover of major magazines, including Vogue, and a feature interview in Glamour.

During the beginning months of the Bush administration, missile defense was a primary foreign policy concern. Throughout his presidential campaign, Bush noted the need for a strategic defense initiative that would protect the United States against what he referred to as rogue states. This was due, in part, to the influence of a special group Secretary of Defense Donald Rumsfeld assembled in 1999–2000 to study possibilities for missile defense, which they considered to be Reagan's unfulfilled legacy (Mann, 2004). There were overlaps between Rumsfeld's group and The Vulcans.

Stephen Hadley, one of the Vulcans who later became Rice's deputy director of the National Security Council, and Rumsfeld were both strong advocates for moving forward with missile defense (Grossman and Long, 2001).

Missile defense was a controversial issue because it would mean that the United States would break with the Anti-Ballistic Missile Treaty, which was signed in 1972 by Cold War superpowers. The purpose of the treaty was to guarantee that the United States and the Soviet Union would not develop or deploy systems that would protect against intercontinental ballistic missiles; instead, the treaty was based on a theory of "mutually assured destruction," or MAD. This was considered to be a major deterrent from launching nuclear arms in the first place. Throughout the beginning of the administration's first term, Rice spent a considerable amount of time assuring the American public and the world that changes to the Anti-Ballistic Missile Treaty would only happen in consultation with Russia and China. On ABC's *This Week* program in May, 2001, Rice said, "U.S. missile defense plans still are at an early stage, with no one ready yet to suggest 'an architecture' for the system." She went on to explain that this was why it was a perfect time for consultations with "friends and allies and with the Russians and with the Chinese about how we move forward." (as quoted in Eichler, 2001)

A second foreign policy concern for the new administration was the Powell Doctrine. General Colin Powell popularized this during the 1990–1991 run-up to the first Gulf War. Influenced by his experiences in the Vietnam War, he felt that the United States should go to war only under certain very stringent conditions. Then, when at war, the U.S. foreign policy should be "First we're going to cut it off, then we're going to kill it." This expression was incorporated into a military policy wherein full military force was used to win a war, and then a quick exit strategy was employed (rather than occupying a nation as peacekeepers). When Rice began her work as national security advisor, she seemed to be intent on upholding this policy. However, by Bush's second year in office, the Powell doctrine seemed to give way to a Rice Doctrine, which was summarized in the 2002 national security strategy as "The aim of U.S. foreign policy ... is to help make the world not just safer, but better." (Preble, 2005, p. 45) This implied a different approach from the Powell Doctrine but, as Preble pointed out, it was not wildly different from any post-Cold War administration's view of foreign policy.

President Bush came to rely on Rice as a confidante; she was clearly among his inner circle. The president knew that he could vent his frustrations and concerns to Rice and that she was able to handle it. He said, "[Rice's] job is to bear the brunt of some of the fire … and she's good at that…. I can be totally unscripted or unrehearsed with Condi. That's the nature of her job, is to absorb my—is to help, you know, kind of say, well, Mr. President I appreciate that point of view, and I think you probably ought to think this way a little bit." (Woodward, 2002, p. 158) Since Rice's office was in the West Wing just a few feet away from the Oval Office, she was able to meet with the president at a moment's notice.

Rice's first major international challenge as national security advisor occurred on April 1, 2001, when a U.S. Navy EP-3 reconnaissance plane was forced to make an emergency landing in China after it "bumped" a Chinese F-8 fighter plane sent to intercept it, forcing the Chinese plane into the sea and killing its pilot. The U.S. plane, loaded with intelligence-gathering equipment, landed on Hainan Island in the South China Sea without advance warning, and its 24-member crew spent 11 days in China before being released. China wanted a formal apology from the United States before it would release the crew members.

This was certainly the most serious military confrontation between China and the United States in more than 30 years (Mann, 2004). There was a great deal of tension as members of the Bush administration recognized the possibility of war or economic problems in light of the event. Rice was instrumental in helping the president with the delicate negotiations to secure the release of the flight crew. U.S. Ambassador to China Joseph Prueher worked with administration officials to craft and deliver a letter expressing that the United States was "very sorry" for the loss of the Chinese pilot and for landing in China without official approval. After this, Chinese officials released the crew members and the crisis seemed to ease.

Throughout the spring and summer of 2001, Rice's schedule included almost daily meetings with George Tenet of the CIA, and she generally spoke with Rumsfeld and Powell each morning around 7:15. In light of the continued threats posed by Al-Qaeda, Rice worked with the administration to develop a new and comprehensive strategy to eliminate that terrorist group. President Bush approved and signed the new strategy on September 4, 2001. The directive ordered departments within the U.S. government to make the elimination of Al-Qaeda a top priority, and delegated specific responsibilities to particular members of the administration to freeze assets and disrupt Al-Qaeda training activities. This counterterrorism strategy included plans for working with other countries in the region (see The White House, 2004 for more details). Unfortunately, the plan was not developed or implemented in time to thwart the tragic events that occurred on September 11, just seven days after it was approved.

SEPTEMBER 11, 2001

Rice was in Washington on the morning of September 11, 2001. At 8:45 A.M. the first plane crashed into the north tower of the World Trade Center. A few minutes later, a second plane slammed into the south tower. Then a third plane flew into the Pentagon, and a fourth went down in a field in rural Pennsylvania. Some speculated that this fourth plane was really intended to hit the White House or the Capitol building, and that it was only the brave actions of the passengers on board the plane that prevented this from happening. More than 3,000 American citizens died in this unprecedented attack on the United States.

Talk show host Oprah Winfrey asked Rice where she was at the time of the attacks. Rice explained, "I was at my ·desk in the White House at around 8:45, when my executive assistant came in and said a plane had hit the World Trade Center. I thought, 'What a strange accident!' I called the president in Florida and said, 'Mr. President, a plane hit the World Trade Center.' And he said, 'What a weird accident.' Around nine, after I went to a staff meeting, my assistant handed me a paper that said a second plane had hit the World Trade Center, and I thought, 'My God, this is a terrorist attack!'" (Ditchfield, 2003, p. 84). Rice went to the Situation Room to organize a meeting. Then the third plane hit the Pentagon, and a false report circulated about a car bomb going off at the State Department. After speaking to the president on the telephone about his return to the White House, Rice went to the underground bunker called the PEOC—the Presidential Emergency Operations Center—where Vice President Cheney was waiting. The vice president's wife Lynne was there, as was Scooter Libby, the vice president's advisor. The bunker is a secure location in the basement of the West Wing, one that would be used by the Bush family and members of the administration over the next weeks and years as various threats against the White House continued to be made.

On September 11, members of the administration operated from the bunker as they waited for the president's return. President Bush, who had been at the Emma E. Booker Elementary School in Sarasota, Florida when the second plane crashed into the World Trade Center, was being shuffled from one part of the country to another to avoid alleged threats to the presidential plane, Air Force One. Air Force One flew to Barksdale Air Force base in Louisiana and Offutt Air Force Base in Nebraska before returning Bush to Washington on the evening of September 11.

By 10:00 A.M. on September 11, Rice was safely inside the White House bunker. She sat next to Vice President Cheney and listened as the vice president talked with President Bush on the telephone. Rice also called her aunt and uncle in Birmingham to let them know that she was fine (they were the closest family members she had since her father passed away nearly a year earlier) (Ditchfield, 2003). Then she began to telephone governments around the world to assure them that the U.S. government was still functioning. Other members of the administration were trying to travel back to the United States after they heard about the attacks. General Colin Powell made his way back from Peru; Treasury Secretary Paul O'Neill returned from Tokyo.

Some felt the terrorist attacks of September 11, 2001 should not have been a surprise to Rice or members of the Bush administration. George Tenet, CIA director, had sent her a memo August 6, 2001 warning of an attack. Richard Clarke, a national security expert, claimed he sent a memo to Rice warning of domestic terror threats. Senator Gary Hart, who knew Rice personally from her work on his campaign in the 1980s, claimed to have offered warnings to her and others in the administration of an impending attack on the American homeland. Hart was co-chair (with Senator Warren Rudman) of the U.S. Commission on National Security, and the two had led a bipartisan group for more than two years of the Clinton administration to study and review security issues. Among their recommendations had been to create a Department of Homeland Security, something the Bush administration ignored until eight months after the September 11 attacks. Hart even met personally with Rice on September 6, 2001 to urge more immediate attention to this issue.

Up until the day of the September 11 attacks, missile defense had been the top defense priority for Rice and Bush. No public statements Rice made before the September 11 attacks mentioned Al-Qaeda, and only once did she mention Osama bin Laden (see http://www.americanprogress.org for further analysis of these claims). After the attacks, this all changed dramatically.

WAR ON TERROR

As Rice had pointed out in her 1984 book on the Czechloslovak army, "[A]s the Chinese characters for crisis (wei-ji) indicate, crises contain both danger (wei) and opportunity (ji)." (Rice, 1984, p. 3). In the September 11 crisis and its aftermath, Rice and the Bush administration saw both danger and opportunity. On one hand, they knew the United States and its military would be at risk and that people would die. At the same time, they wondered if this would be an opportunity to forge new relations with Russia and China (Woodward, 2002). Perhaps they saw opportunities for a different U.S. presence in the Middle East.

The Bush Doctrine, "Go after the terrorists and those who harbor them," was announced on the evening of September 11, 2001. In his seven-minute speech to the public from the Oval Office, Bush explained the tough line Americans would take in response to the terrorist attacks. He had spent the day consulting with presidential counselor Karen Hughes, Condoleezza Rice, and other key members of his staff. At one point, he was unsure whether to include the statement "We will make no distinction between those who planned these attacks and those who harbor them." Rice advised him that he would have other opportunities to say this, but she did feel that the first words from the president would matter the most, and in the end favored including this sentence (Woodward, 2002).

After the speech, Bush gathered his most senior NSC staff in the White House bunker. He further discussed with his advisors the need to punish those who harbor terrorists, not just the terrorists alone. It was one of the most significant foreign policy decisions in American history, and Rice was central in supporting the administration's determination to go forward with this policy.

Rice spent the night of September 11 in residential quarters of the White House. Although she was assigned a Secret Service detail, the administration felt it was too dangerous for her to return to her Watergate Hotel apartment. She agreed to stay at the White House bunker but the Bushes insisted that she should stay with them, instead. Their residence would be much more comfortable. She didn't return to her apartment until the third night after the crisis, and she slept only fitfully. When she finally returned home, she turned her television on and saw the changing of the guard in front of Buckingham Palace; the Coldstream Guards were playing "The Star Spangled Banner" as a demonstration of solidarity with the United States. Rice wept (Woodward, 2002).

On September 14, Rice joined Rumsfeld, Cheney, and Powell at Camp David. The president arrived later than the others and they spent Saturday, September 15 in discussions with members of the War Cabinet about how they should respond to the attacks. During these meetings, Rice expressed concern about the potential for the United States to be caught in a quagmire in Afghanistan, and she agreed with Vice President Cheney that they needed to tread carefully in their relations with Pakistan. Rice kept Iraq in the discussions as they considered the possibility of successful military operations beyond Afghanistan (Woodward, 2002).

After lunch, Rice met briefly with Powell, Rumsfeld, Tenet, and White House Chief of Staff Andy Card, and then she exercised for a short time before the meetings reconvened around 4:00 P.M. When the session began, Bush asked the attendees to explain their positions. He started with Powell and then moved around the table. He asked Rice to listen, which she did. As the meeting ended, the president promised to mull over the options. Later that evening, Rice invited the others to go bowling. When no one accepted her offer, she led the group in singing some American standard songs and patriotic tunes. Notably absent were Powell and Rumsfeld, who left Camp David when the meeting concluded (Suskind, 2004).

The days following the September 11 attacks were tumultuous, to say the least. There were meetings to attend and important decisions to make as threats from credible sources continued against the White House and the United States. Intelligence officials attempted to sort through various leads and information to find the perpetrators of the attacks. Security team members discussed how to mobilize the military, how to secure support from Uzbekistan so its airspace could be utilized in the counterattacks, and how to offer humanitarian aid in the wake of the counterattacks. They were well aware of the anti-American sentiment in various parts of the world and they were concerned about biological warfare. These were surely difficult days for Rice as she negotiated with members of the team and worked to answer the president's questions about when the military counterattacks could begin.

Within days, the administration determined that Osama bin Laden and the Al-Qaeda terrorist network were responsible for the terrorist attacks. Al Qaeda's base was in Afghanistan, where the fundamentalist Islamic leadership, the Taliban, was sympathetic to its cause. The Bush administration offered an ultimatum to the Taliban: Al-Qaeda leaders had to be delivered to the United States; all imprisoned foreign nationals had to be released; foreign journalists, diplomats, and aid workers had to be protected; all terrorist training camps had to be closed; and the United States had to be given access to terrorist training camps to verify they were closed. Taliban leaders offered their response to Bush through the Pakistan embassy, demanding evidence of bin Laden's involvement in the attacks and offering to try him in an Islamic court. The U.N. Security Council also issued a resolution demanding bin Laden's capture and that all terrorist camps be closed. Many leaders of foreign countries offered their support to the United States and individuals from around the world sent their condolences.

U.S. military strikes against Afghanistan began on October 7, 2001. Afghanistan, which is geographically the size of the state of Texas, is 7,000 miles from the United States and has a population of 26 million people. On the first night of bombing, U.S. and British missiles hit 40 planned targets, including the airport and sites in the cities of Kabul (Afghanistan's capital) Kandahar, and Jalalabad. Eventually, 7,000 U.S. troops would enter the country to fight in the war. The military initiative was dubbed Operation Enduring Freedom, but many questioned the need to launch attacks that would most certainly bring more death, particularly to innocent civilians. In New York City on the day the bombing began, approximately 10,000 to 12,000 people marched for peace, while about 100,000 took to the streets in London for the same cause. Many people felt the United States had missed an opportunity to be a leader in world peace, and some even criticized Rice personally. Alan Gilbert, Rice's former professor at the University of Denver, argued that Rice and the Bush administration had lost their way (Gilbert, 2002). While Gilbert remembered Rice as a thoughtful and bold student, he argued that the administration's aggression and belligerence did not make the world a safer place.

The campaign in Afghanistan also had no clear ending point. This was something the administration officials had discussed from the outset but it remained an issue they could not resolve. How would they know when they accomplished their goal against terrorism, particularly when the enemy was so difficult to identify and find? Early in their discussions, the security team was clear that they wanted to avoid a quagmire, they wanted to avoid another Vietnam, and they wanted to avoid nation-building. Rather than moving away from these concerns, however, they seemed to gain momentum toward them, particularly when they considered Iraq.

WAR IN IRAQ

Although rice had focused primarily on Russia and China, Iraq was a topic she brought up in her discussions with Bush when she was his foreign policy advisor during the run-up to the 2000 presidential campaign (Woodward, 2002). In their talks, Bush was clear that he felt his father and his father's administration did the right thing by ending the first Gulf War when they did. However, Bush also felt that there were problems in Iraq that still needed to be resolved. He considered the country to be a rogue state that posed threats to the United States and the world. Bush and his advisors did not feel the U.N. weapons inspectors and the sanctions imposed on Iraq after the first Gulf War had been adequate to prevent Iraq's presumed proliferation of biological and chemical weapons.

In the aftermath of the September 11 attacks, talks among the advisors changed. Iraq was frequently brought up in National Security Council meetings as the members discussed the war on terror. Rice, Rumsfeld, and Cheney all felt something needed to be done about Saddam Hussein, as did presidential advisor Karl Rove. General Powell, who was secretary of defense during the first Gulf War, was not as convinced but he did not publicly dissent from the administration's message. The administration made it clear to the American public that Saddam Hussein had weapons of mass destruction and Iraq was a threat that needed to addressed.

By the time of President Bush's second State of the Union address in January, 2002, it was clear to the American public that Iraq was a priority for the administration. During his speech, Bush discussed what he called the axis of evil—Iraq, Iran, and North Korea—and his growing concern about the accumulation of weapons of mass destruction. He explained:

Our second goal is to prevent regimes that sponsor terror from threatening America or our friends and allies with weapons of mass destruction. Some of these regimes have been pretty quiet since September the 11th. But we know their true nature. North Korea is a regime arming with missiles and weapons of mass destruction, while starving its citizens.

Iran aggressively pursues these weapons and exports terror, while an unelected few repress the Iranian people's hope for freedom.

Iraq continues to flaunt its hostility toward America and to support terror. The Iraqi regime has plotted to develop anthrax, and nerve gas, and nuclear weapons for over a decade. This is a regime that has already used poison gas to murder thousands of its own citizens—leaving the bodies of mothers huddled over their dead children. This is a regime that agreed to international inspections—then kicked out the inspectors. This is a regime that has something to hide from the civilized world. States like these, and their terrorist allies, constitute an axis of evil, arming to threaten the peace of the world. By seeking weapons of mass destruction, these regimes pose a grave and growing danger. They could provide these arms to terrorists, giving them the means to match their hatred. They could attack our allies or attempt to blackmail the United States. In any of these cases, the price of indifference would be catastrophic.

We will work closely with our coalition to deny terrorists and their state sponsors the materials, technology, and expertise to make and deliver weapons of mass destruction. We will develop and deploy effective missile defenses to protect America and our allies from sudden attack. And all nations should know: America will do what is necessary to ensure our nation's security.

We'll be deliberate, yet time is not on our side. I will not wait on events, while dangers gather. I will not stand by, as peril draws closer and closer. The United States of America will not permit the world's most dangerous regimes to threaten us with the world's most destructive weapons. (Bush, 2002)

In many ways, this speech made public the administration's intentions with regard to foreign policy, national security, and Iraq.

Late in the spring of 2002, General Powell began to request weekly private meetings with President Bush. Rice generally sat in on these meetings, and she also joined Powell and Bush when they met in the president's private residence to discuss the possibility of invading Iraq (Woodward, 2002). Powell had clear concerns about the consequences of such action, based on his own systematic analysis of the problems this military action could bring as well as his extensive experiences with the U.S. military that began during the Vietnam War. Powell made a strong case to the president about the need for coalition-building if there was to be any action against Iraq, and Rice agreed.

By this point in her tenure as national security advisor, Rice was receiving mixed reviews from the general public. On one hand, people generally seemed to respect her intelligence and accomplishments, but many questioned why she was so loyal to the Bush administration and its policies. Nowhere was this more evident than at Stanford University. Rice had been invited to speak at the May, 2002 commencement, and her invitation was met with protest among the student body. Over 3,500 commencement flyers were distributed to those who attended the graduation ceremony. The flyers presented the student complaints against Rice in relation to her years as Stanford provost and National Security Advisor. Many who attended the ceremonies held protest banners throughout the ceremony. Community members and students alike participated in expressing their concerns about Rice's tenure as provost and national security advisor (see Appendix 2 for the commencement flyer distributed at graduation).

On September 8, 2002, Rice was making her usual appearances on Sunday morning news programs. During an interview with CNN's

Wolf Blitzer, Rice continued to make her case for war against Iraq. She explained, "The problem here is that there will always be some uncertainty about how quickly [Saddam Hussein] can acquire nuclear weapons. But we don't want the smoking gun to be a mushroom cloud" (CNN, 2002). This statement made headlines around the world as many shuddered to think of the possibilities of Saddam Hussein launching a nuclear attack. In the months that followed, this was a much-quoted and later a much-criticized statement.

President Bush addressed the U. N. General Assembly on September 12, 2002, just a year after the World Trade Center attacks, to make a case against Iraq and to insist that the U.N. get involved in ways that Saddam Hussein could not ignore. After this speech, General Colin Powell met with members of the U.N. to craft a resolution about what should happen in Iraq. This resolution (No. 1441) passed unanimously on November 12, 2002. This was no small matter, given the reluctance of Germany and France to support any force or threat of force against Iraq. The resolution called for Iraq to admit U.N. weapons inspectors who would search for weapons of mass destruction and destroy any that were found. At the end of the resolution was a warning to Iraq that it would face serious consequences if it violated the resolution (Steins, 2003).

At the end of 2002, weapons inspectors entered Iraq. While the French, Germans, and Russians insisted that the process be given more time, the Americans and the British were clearly frustrated by the process and felt they were being deceived and tricked by the Iraqis. Rice met with French officials, including diplomatic advisor Maurice Gourdault-Montagne. Gourdault-Montagne warned that the war could be dangerous and that it would likely destabilize the Mideast. Rice rejected his arguments, insisting that Saddam Hussein was too much of a threat (Mann, 2004).

On January 23, 2003, Rice wrote an editorial for the *New York Times* entitled "Why We Know Iraq is Lying." In it, she made the case for war in Iraq clear to the American people. She wrote:

> Instead of a commitment to disarm, Iraq has a high-level political commitment to maintain and conceal its weapons, led by Saddam Hussein and his son Qusay, who controls the Special Security Organization, which runs Iraq's concealment activities. Instead of implementing national initiatives to disarm, Iraq maintains institutions whose sole purpose is to thwart the work of the inspectors. And instead of full cooperation and transparency, Iraq has filed a false declaration to the United Nations that amounts to a 12,200-page lie.... Iraq's declaration even resorted to unabashed

plagiarism, with lengthy passages of United Nations reports copied word-for-word (or edited to remove any criticism of Iraq) and presented as original text. Far from informing, the declaration is intended to cloud and confuse the true picture of Iraq's arsenal. It is a reflection of the regime's well-earned reputation for dishonesty and constitutes a material breach of United Nations Security Council Resolution 1441, which set up the current inspections program.... By both its actions and its inactions, Iraq is proving not that it is a nation bent on disarmament, but that it is a nation with something to hide. Iraq is still treating inspections as a game. It should know that time is running out. (Rice, 2003)

Rice consistently repeated this message to the press and the American public in the months leading up to the Iraq war.

The United States and Great Britain went before the U.N. to obtain approval for their plans to invade Iraq, but the French, Germans, and Russians could not be convinced to support any act of force against the Iraqis. Because a new resolution to use force would not be passed by the U.N. Security Council, the Americans and the British decided they would rely on the language of Resolution 1441, and that the language of "serious consequences" would allow them to militarily invade Iraq to seek out the weapons of mass destruction (Steins, 2003). The United States and Great Britain preemptively attacked Iraq on March 26, 2003, three months and three days after Rice's editorial appeared in *The New York Times*. The United States and Great Britain had no support from their allies; this act would dramatically change the course of U.S. foreign policy.

The Iraq invasion in March, 2003 was highly controversial, even within the ranks of the Republican Party. Rice's former boss, Brent Scowcroft, was among the most vocal of critics (Kessler, 2004). He wanted to clearly separate the war in Afghanistan, which had direct links to the September 11 attacks, from the invasion of Iraq, which had no direct connections to Osama bin Laden and the Al-Qaeda network. Scowcroft was concerned that military action in Iraq would increase hatred and suspicion toward the United States among the Arab nations. Scowcroft, General Wesley Clark, and others who opposed the Iraq war were often interviewed on television news programs, and Rice spent a great deal of time appearing on similar broadcasts to convince the American people that the war was the right thing to do.

Once troops were mobilized to Iraq, American forces moved quickly toward Baghdad. Under the command of General Tommy Franks, American soldiers engaged in armed conflict in Iraqi cities that included

Basra, Nassiriya, Najaf, and Mosul. On April 9, 2003, Baghdad fell to coalition forces. Media around the world showed images of soldiers toppling statues of Saddam Hussein and occupying his many ornate palaces around the city. Tikrit, Saddam Hussein's hometown, came under the control of American forces on April 13, with little resistance offered by the Iraqis. On April 15, 2003, American and British forces declared that the war was over. Troops remained in Iraq and the period of coalition occupation began.

One problem Rice and the Bush administration faced after the invasion of Iraq was how to reconstitute the Iraqi military. Rice had studied problems of rebuilding militaries in the context of Eastern Europe after World War II (Rice, 1984). In particular, she studied how the Soviet military influenced and controlled the military in Czechoslovakia, and she noted how there were tensions in the civil–military relations because the armed forces needed to serve both Czechoslovakia and the Soviet Union.

Another problem was the increasing pressure to explain why the United States had gone to war. As months passed and no weapons of mass destruction were found, questions about faulty intelligence information surfaced. While Rice's role as national security advisor in the midst of this intelligence problem was questioned, criticisms of her did not seem to take hold (Mann, 2004). Nevertheless, she was still required to testify before a panel of prominent legislators who were charged with investigating the problems with U.S. intelligence prior to the September 11 attacks.

TESTIMONY BEFORE THE 9/11 COMMISSION

On November 27, 2002, Congress and President Bush created an independent, bipartisan panel to investigate and report a complete account of the events surrounding the terrorist attacks of September 11, 2001. The National Commission on Terrorist Attacks on the United States (also called the 9/11 Commission) was also charged with providing recommendations that would guard against future terrorist attacks (see http://www.9-11commission.gov/ for more detailed information on the commission and its work). President Bush initially allocated $3 million for the investigation; later, the commission requested an additional $8 million. Critics felt this was an inadequate amount of money, particularly when compared with federal dollars spent on other national disasters. For example, the investigation into the 1986 space shuttle Challenger catastrophe was given $50 million (Griffin, 2004).

The committee had 80 full-time employees on staff. To organize its work, the commission was divided into the following focus areas: Al-Qaeda and the Organization of the 9/11 Attack; Intelligence Collection, Analysis, and Management (including oversight and resource allocation); International Counterterrorism Policy, including states that harbor or harbored terrorists, or offer or offered terrorists safe havens; Terrorist Financing; Border Security and Foreign Visitors; Law Enforcement and Intelligence Collection inside the United States; Commercial Aviation and Transportation Security, including an Investigation into the Circumstances of the Four Hijackings; and The Immediate Response to the Attacks at the National, State, and Local levels, including issues of Continuity of Government.

Ten commissioners led the investigation. At first, the White House appointed former Secretary of State Henry Kissinger to lead the commission. However, Kissinger drew much criticism because of questions about his role in past government cover-ups, and he resigned the post. After Kissinger stepped down, Thomas Kean, former New Jersey governor and president of Drew University, chaired the committee, and Lee Hamilton, a former Congressman from Indiana, served as vice chair. Philip Zelikow, Rice's former colleague and co-editor, served as executive director.

The committee reviewed presidential daily briefs (PDBs) and members used subpoenas to access information from the Federal Aviation Administration (FAA), the Department of Defense, and the City of New York. Over two and a half million pages of documents were considered. In addition, members interviewed more than 1,000 individuals in 10 countries around the world, and they held 10 days of public hearings where more than 110 federal, state, and local officials, as well as members of the public sector, were interviewed. Some of the more prominent public figures interviewed during the public hearings included Richard Armitage, Donald Rumsfeld, Colin Powell, Paul Wolfowitz, Richard Clarke, former Defense Secretary William Cohen, former Secretary of State Madeleine Albright, and former National Security Advisor Sandy Berger.

As the commission's work got underway, there was a great deal of speculation about who would be interviewed from the Bush administration. The president and vice president agreed to meet privately with Chairman Kean and Vice Chairman Hamilton, but the commission hoped that Bush and Cheney would meet with all members. Eventually, Bush and Cheney did meet privately with the commission but only under specific conditions: they testified jointly; they did not take an oath; the testimony was not recorded; and notes of the testimony would not be made public. The commission agreed to these conditions, and on April 29, 2004, Bush and Cheney offered their testimony in a private meeting.

At first, the Bush administration refused to allow Rice to engage in public testimony. Never before had a sitting national security advisor testified in public hearings of this nature. Instead of participating in a public hearing, Rice met privately with the commission on February 7, 2004, but this did not seem to satisfy the commissioners. They continued to press for Rice to engage in a public testimony.

On March 22, 2004, Rice penned an editorial for *The Washington Post* entitled "9/11: For the Record." In this editorial, she explained that Al-Qaeda had been a threat to the United States for more than a decade and that the U.S. government, including the Clinton and Bush administrations, had worked very hard during this decade to counter those threats. She explained that the Bush administration took these threats seriously, and among the administration's efforts to thwart this threat was funding for counterterrorism and intelligence efforts, and that they pursued Al-Qaeda's funding sources. Rice noted that efforts were made during the spring and summer of 2001 to develop a strategy to eliminate Al-Qaeda. She explained that President Bush met with CIA Director George Tenet each day and that she attended these meetings. Rice maintained that the administration had received only vague threats and that there was no way to predict the events of September 11:

> Despite what some have suggested, we received no intelligence that terrorists were preparing to attack the homeland using airplanes as missiles, though some analysts speculated that terrorists might hijack airplanes to try to free U.S.-held terrorists. "The FAA even issued a warning to airlines and aviation security personnel that 'the potential for a terrorist operation, such as an airline hijacking to free terrorists incarcerated in the United States, remains a concern.'" (Rice, 2004)

Rice received a great deal of criticism for this statement because some felt there had, in fact, been sufficient evidence that airplanes would be used as missiles to attack the United States. However, Rice did not change her position in relation to this claim.

On March 30, 2004, White House Counsel Alberto Gonzales wrote a letter to Commissioner Kean expressing the administration's reservations about having a sitting national security advisor testify in public hearings. In spite of their concerns, the administration agreed to allow Rice to testify at the public hearing, but only under the following conditions:

First, the Commission must agree in writing that Dr. Rice's testimony before the Commission does not set any precedent for future Commission requests or requests in any other context for testimony by a National Security Advisor or any other White House official.

Second, the Commission must agree in writing that it will not request additional public testimony from any White House official, including Dr. Rice. The National Security Advisor is uniquely situated to provide the Commission with information necessary to fulfill its statutory mandate. Indeed, it is for this reason that Dr. Rice privately met with the Commission for more than four hours on February 7, fully answered every question posed to her, and offered additional private meetings as necessary. Despite the fact that the Commission will therefore have access to all information of which Dr. Rice is aware, the Commission has nevertheless urged that public confidence in the work of the Commission would be enhanced by Dr. Rice appearing publicly before the Commission. (Gonzalez, 2004)

In conversations on news programs and with the media, Rice expressed her interest in testifying in a public hearing before the commission but, consistent with Gonzalez, she maintained that it could set a problematic precedent to have a sitting national security advisor engage in public testimony.

Amid increasing pressure from the commission, the public, and family members of victims of the September 11 attacks, Rice finally offered public testimony about September 11. On April 8, 2004, Rice sat poised before the commission and the American public. She articulately offered opening remarks in which she conveyed the sorrow and anger she felt in relation to the terrorist attacks, but she stopped short of offering any apology. Instead, she provided some context for the attacks and some hint of what was to come in terms of the Bush administration's foreign policy toward terrorists:

The terrorists were at war with us, but we were not yet at war with them. For more than 20 years, the terrorist threat gathered, and America's response across several administrations of both parties was insufficient. Historically, democratic societies have been slow to react to gathering threats, tending instead to wait to confront threats until they are too dangerous to ignore or until it is too late. Despite the sinking of the *Lusitania* in 1915 and continued

German harassment of American shipping, the United States did not enter the First World War until two years later. Despite Nazi Germany's repeated violations of the Versailles Treaty and its string of provocations throughout the mid-1930s, the Western democracies did not take action until 1939. The U.S. Government did not act against the growing threat from Imperial Japan until the threat became all too evident at Pearl Harbor. And, tragically, for all the language of war spoken before September 11th, this country simply was not on a war footing. Since then, America has been at war. And under President Bush's leadership, we will remain at war until the terrorist threat to our Nation is ended. The world has changed so much that it is hard to remember what our lives were like before that day. But I do want to describe the actions this Administration was taking to fight terrorism before September 11th, 2001 ... President Bush had set a broad foreign policy agenda. We were determined to confront the proliferation of weapons of mass destruction. We were improving America's relations with the world's great powers. We had to change an Iraq policy that was making no progress against a hostile regime which regularly shot at U.S. planes enforcing U.N. Security Council Resolutions. And we had to deal with the occasional crisis, for instance, when the crew of a Navy plane was detained in China for 11 days. We also moved to develop a new and comprehensive strategy to eliminate the al-Qaida terrorist network. President Bush understood the threat, and he understood its importance. (Rice, 2004, April 8)

There were moments in Rice's testimony when commission members pressed her for further information. Richard Ben-Veniste insisted on more information from an August, 2001 memo to the president that Rice recalled was entitled "Bin Laden Determined to Attack Inside the United States." Although Rice insisted that the memo contained no information about attacks inside the United States or that terrorists would use airplanes as missiles, Ben-Veniste insisted that the memo be declassified, noting that even the title of the document was a secret up to that point. Members in the audience applauded when Ben-Veniste pressed this issue and other members of the commission supported his call for declassification of the memo.

Rice's testimony before the commission lasted for three hours. Rice and Ben-Veniste clashed a few times during the testimony and he later complained on MSNBC's *Countdown* that he could not get Rice to answer his questions frankly. Former Senator Bob Kerrey, a commission member, also sharply criticized Rice and the Bush administration during Rice's testimony. When Rice stated that Bush did not want to respond to Al-Qaeda attacks one at a time because he was "tired of swatting flies," Kerrey replied sharply. He said, "Dr. Rice, we only swatted a fly once…. How the hell could he [Bush] be tired?" In spite of their harsh exchanges, Kerrey and Rice contributed a few light moments in the midst of the serious proceedings. When Kerrey repeatedly referred to Rice as Dr. Clarke, Rice responded, "Sir, with all respect, I don't think I look like Dick Clarke" (MSNBC and NBC News, 2004).

When Rice's testimony was finished, she left Washington for Crawford, Texas to spend Easter weekend with the president and First Lady at their ranch. Bush's twin daughters Jenna and Barbara were there, along with Laura Bush's mother, Jenna Welch, and the president's parents. On Easter Sunday, Rice joined Bush and his family as they made a quick visit to Fort Hood to express their support to the soldiers stationed at the army base well. Nine soldiers from the base were killed in Iraq during the week before Easter and 31 were injured in Baghdad.

On July 22, 2004, the commission's findings were published in a book made available to the general public on web sites and in bookstores. In the book, the commission concluded that the September 11 terrorist attacks were a shock but, given the amount of warning from bin Laden and his terrorist networks, they should not have been a surprise. The commission identified the administration's greatest failure as one of imagination. Commissioners felt the administration did not fully appreciate the gravity of the threat bin Laden posed and, consequently, the administration did not address this threat through policy. The commission identified management issues among top leaders of the country, including problems of pooling intelligence across agencies such as the CIA, the FBI, the State Department, the military, and other groups associated with homeland security. The commission's recommendations were in three general areas: (1) attack terrorists and their organizations; (2) prevent the continued growth of Islamic terrorism; and (3) protect against and prepare for terrorist attacks.

After the commission's work was published, Margaret Warner of the Public Broadcasting Service's *NewsHour* interviewed Rice. She asked one question about the personal responsibility Rice may have felt in the aftermath of the attacks. Rice replied:

> Well, of course. We all, I think all of us who had anything to do with national security over the period of time in which this threat grew, which is—by the way—not just the 90s; we tend to think

about 1993 and the World Trade Center bombing and al-Qaida, but I've heard former Secretary of State George Shultz give a very impressive speech about how he thinks about how they might have differently thought about the Marine barracks bombing in 1982 in Lebanon, or how we might have thought about a follow-on, a series of terrorist attacks against us that clearly showed that this was building up, and it's very often the case for democracies—and I made this point to the commission—that we don't see a threat materialize until it's already too late…. I think the one thing that September 11 has taught us is to not let threats materialize or fully materialize[,] that you have to take care of them as they're gathering, not when you finally have an attack as a result of them. (NewsHour, 2004)

Rice's message about September 11 and its aftermath remained consistent as she stood firm in her support for President Bush and his policies.

BEYOND FOREIGN AFFAIRS

As national security advisor, Rice was sometimes mentioned in relation to issues that extended beyond foreign affairs, particularly issues related to race and racism in the United States. On more than one occasion, Rice was drawn into conversations about race and racism. Rice understood what it was like to be discriminated against because of race. Even as a member of Scowcroft's national security team, she experienced racism. In 1990 she was leading a contingent of delegates to accompany Mikhail Gorbachev on a tour across the United States, and a Secret Service agent who obviously did not know who Rice was stopped her as she stepped onto the tarmac at the San Francisco airport (Felix, 2002).

Rice also knew what it meant to benefit from affirmative action policies. Her initial fellowship position at Stanford University was paid for with funds for minority faculty and her professorship was created for her without the usual national search process. Journalist Nicholas Lemann (2002) asked former Stanford President Gerhard Casper whether race or gender had anything to do with appointing Rice as provost. Casper replied, "It would be disingenuous for me to say that the fact that she was a woman, the fact that she was black, and the fact that she was young weren't in my mind. They were."

Although Rice had experienced racism first-hand as a child and adult, and while she experienced the benefits of affirmative action, she refused to attribute racism to every insult or privilege she or others may experience (Ditchfield, 2003). Rice focused her statements about race and racism on individuals rather than on institutions or structures that perpetuate racism in the United States. Rice once explained:

> I would hope that we would spend our time thinking how to educate black children, particularly black children who are caught in poverty. I would hope that we would spend our time, as the president has said 'turning back the soft bigotry of low expectations' against our children. Slavery is more than 150 years in the past, and yes, there's a continuing stain. I've often said slavery was America's birth defect. It was there from the beginning. But we have to turn now to the present and to the future. I'd rather be a minority in this country than in anyplace else in the world. (Ditchfield, 2003, p. 96)

Rice's perspectives on race and blackness were certainly influenced by her family and the slavery her forebears experienced:

> I think that black Americans of my grandparents' ilk had liberated themselves .... They had broken the code. They had figured out how to make an extraordinarily comfortable and fulfilling life despite the circumstances. They did not feel that they were captives.... It isn't an immigrant story. It's a different story.... We have a language for dealing with immigration, but not with race, where we came to this country together but with blacks enslaved. I often talk about how when America was founded it had a birth defect, with slavery. It was there from the beginning.... I know the motivation for 'African American' was to connect black Americans with the African heritage, and that part I applaud.... But it implies a pure connection to Africa that doesn't go through the experiences of slavery or a mixing of the blood. (Russakoff, 2001)

Rice has been criticized for not aggressively supporting affirmative action, particularly when President Bush engaged in discussions about the University of Michigan's admissions policy in 2003. Instead, she remained consistent in her position that individuals can overcome public problems, such as racism, through education and perseverance.

HER 50TH BIRTHDAY PARTY

Rice marked an important milestone in her personal life when she was national security advisor. On November 14, 2004, Rice turned 50. She had expected to celebrate her birthday by quietly eating dinner with her Aunt G (Genoa Ray McPhatter) and a few friends. As the two headed for their destination in a Secret Service limo, Rice noticed that the driver changed course. When the limo stopped in front of British ambassador David Manning's residence, Rice knew something was going on. The two women entered the residence to applause, cheers, and a rendition of "Happy Birthday" sung by more than a hundred friends who gathered to surprise Rice and celebrate her special day. George Schultz, Colin Powell, Sandy Berger, Karen Hughes, Karl Rove, and President Bush and the First Lady were among the guests, as was Rice's frequent companion, NFL executive Gene Washington.

As she acknowledged her guests, Rice exclaimed, "Look what I'm wearing!" (Dowd, 2005). While Rice had a reputation for always being beautifully dressed, she was clearly out of place in her casual slacks and suede jacket. All the guests were in tuxedos or ball gowns, dressed for an elegant, black-tie affair. What Rice did not know was that a beautiful red gown by her favorite designer, Oscar de la Renta, was waiting for her in a nearby room, as was her hair stylist.

In a matter of moments, Rice was transformed into the belle of the ball. She rejoined her friends, who were seated at tables named after Rice's favorite football teams. Pianist Van Cliburn played the national anthem. Rice visited with friends, danced, and enjoyed the evening. For a woman who worked countless hours and had little social entertainment beyond an occasional event at the Kennedy Center or a weekend afternoon watching sports on television, the evening must have felt like a dream.

MOVING TO FRONT AND CENTER

Throughout her term as national security advisor, Rice was clearly among President Bush's inner circle. Few had the attention of the president in ways that Rice commanded. She was his advisor, confidante, and friend. Rice's devout loyalty to the president was repeatedly apparent and she never diverged from the administration's position, even in the midst of intense scrutiny, public interrogation, and international pressure. While the general public was aware of tensions and differences of opinion between the president and Secretary of State Colin Powell, no one could detect any dissent between Bush and Rice. For all intents and purposes, their positions were identical. Rice often said that it was her job to take Bush's instincts and turn them into policy.

As national security advisor during George W. Bush's first term in office, Rice's political conservatism was evident. As Rice began her work for the administration, the Associated Press (2000) noted that she argued against humanitarian missions and international treaties and for a hard line on Russia and putting U.S. strategic interests at the center of all decisions.

In addition to the challenges in Iraq and Afghanistan, other areas of the world presented challenges to Rice and the administration. Israel and Palestine were ongoing sources of concern throughout Rice's tenure as national security advisor, and stabilizing relationships between the Israelis and Palestinians would be a top item on her agenda when she later became secretary of state. In addition, she had to consider carefully how the administration would deal with Iran and North Korea and their pursuit of nuclear weapons. U.S.–China relations posed ongoing puzzles. These areas would demand much attention from Rice as she moved to the front and center of the world stage.

As she proceeded into the second term of the Bush administration, her positions seemed to be solidified, but this had not always been the case. Rice's views on policy issues clearly shifted during Bush's first term. When she spoke at the Republican National Convention in 2000, she explained Bush's position that Americans were at their best when they exercise their power without arrogance or fanfare. However, within a year of that speech, she was clearly aligned with those in the administration who believed preemptive action in Iraq was necessary. Rice, who once noted that political scientist Hans Morgenthau was most influential in her own thinking about foreign policy and international relations, clearly underwent a transformation in her political thought. Morgenthau was a political realist, one who believed that countries should be dealt with on their own terms (in other words, political realists believe there should not be efforts to change the governing structures of other countries). This was why some prominent political realists, such as former National Security Advisor Brent Scowcroft, felt the war in Iraq was wrong. Scowcroft and those who shared his views were skeptical that democracy could grow in Iraq with the United States occupying the country.

Within the context of the George W. Bush administration, Rice seemed to shift away from the influences of Morgenthau, toward moralistic views of foreign policy. In the aftermath of the September 11 attacks, she supported Bush's position that particular universal values needed to be supported by everyone, among them freedom and democracy. In 2002, her office released a "National Security Strategy," which claimed that there is "a single sustainable model for national success—America's—that is 'right and true for every person, in every society'" (Lemann, 2002). The document asserts America's dominance in the world and proclaims that America will not be afraid to act alone to protect its interests.

As the 2004 campaign for the U.S. presidency heated up, Rice campaigned for Bush's re-election. In the weeks before the election, she traveled to key battleground states, including Oregon, Washington, Pennsylvania, Ohio, Michigan, Florida, and North Carolina. Her activity on the campaign trail drew criticism, particularly from those who felt that America's national security advisor should not be overtly involved in presidential campaign. Zbigniew Brzezinski, former National Security Advisor to Jimmy Carter, explained, "That is certainly politicizing the job. I can't speak for the other national security advisors, but my recollection is we viewed the job as not a highly political one, to the extent that's possible being that close to the president" (as quoted in Kessler, 2004, October 20).

When Bush won election to his second term in office, many expected that Rice would be nominated as secretary of state. However, some expressed concern about the breadth of her experience in relation to such an appointment. Brent Scowcroft noted, "She's very good in Russia and the Soviet Union, good in Europe, but it tapers off after that" (as quoted in Kessler, 2005). While she was national security advisor, Rice made just six solo international trips—three to Russia, one to London, one to Asia, and one to the Middle East. But her colleague Coit Blacker and others who knew Rice in her role as provost of Stanford expected she would step seamlessly into her new role as secretary of state, if it was offered to her.

Chapter 6

MADAME SECRETARY

By the time Condoleezza Rice was sworn in as secretary of state on January 28, 2005, she was clearly one of the most powerful women in the world. In fact, she topped the *Forbes* list of one hundred most powerful women, earning this title in 2005. Rice was what many referred to as a rock star politician—a megastar whose name was recognized the world over. She was featured on the covers of magazines and newspapers around the world, and commentators noted her clothing and sense of style as often as they did her politics. When she appeared at the Weisbaden Army Airfield in Germany in her "Matrix-dominatrix" black coat and spike-heeled boots, newspapers and blogs around the world carried pictures of her greeting troops and commented endlessly on her appearance, while barely noting her words to the troops stationed at the base.

Of course, Rice's words still held much sway within the Bush administration and across the world. At Bush's second inauguration, Rice used the term "outposts of tyranny," which seemed to be linked to Bush's earlier phrase "axis of evil." This phrase set the agenda for her work over her first year as secretary of state. Outposts of tyranny referred to those countries that threatened world peace and human rights, those countries where Rice felt the United States had some responsibility for fostering freedom. Specifically, these countries included Cuba, Zimbabwe, Belarus, Iran, North Korea, and Burma. Rice would explicitly address issues in relation to these countries as she traveled the world meeting with presidents, chancellors, foreign secretaries of state, and other leaders. Many people were counting on her tough diplomacy to change America's image and relationships with foreign countries. As Rice stated at her confirmation hearing, "[W]e must use American diplomacy to help create a balance of power in the world that favors freedom. And the time for diplomacy is now." Before this work would begin in earnest, however, she needed to set up her office and appoint the officials who would help to guide her work.

SETTING UP OFFICE

The mission of the office of secretary of state is "to create a more secure, democratic and prosperous world for the benefit of the American people and the international community" (see http://www.state.gov for more information about the office of secretary of state). The strategic plan for the department identifies the following core values as central to the high standards the department plans to achieve:

Loyalty: Commitment to the United States and the American people.

Character: Maintenance of the highest ethical standards and integrity.

Service: Excellence in the formulation of policy and program management with room for creative dissent. Implementation of policy and management practices, regardless of personal views.

Accountability: Responsibility for meeting the highest performance standards.

Community: Dedication to teamwork, professionalism, diversity, and the customer perspective.

The department's web site explains that people are critical to its mission and that mindfulness to history is important, but innovation is also valued, particularly in the challenging times the country is facing.

To accomplish this work, the secretary of state has a significant team of advisors who have specific roles to play in the department. When Condoleezza Rice assembled her team of deputies and advisors in the State Department office, she selected some familiar faces—people who had worked with her extensively before in various government posts, including her counsel Philip Zelikow. Zelikow, Rice's former coauthor, colleague, and director of the 9/11 Commission, would serve as a special advisor to Rice in the State Department. He would be a consultant on major problems of foreign policy and he would provide guidance to Rice on any problems that would arise.

Robert Zoellick would become Rice's deputy secretary of state. He served in the State Department during George H. W. Bush's administration with then-Secretary of State James Baker. Zoellick, who was on the board of Enron Corporation and held other government and business posts throughout his career, was known as an international strategist who had experience working with the World Bank and the World Trade Organization. He had long-standing ties with the Bush family and served as a Vulcan during George W. Bush's first run for the presidency. In this new role with Rice, he would be the principal deputy and advisor to the secretary of state and would serve as the acting secretary of state in Rice's absence.

The undersecretary for political affairs was R. Nicholas Burns. Burns served as the director for Soviet Affairs during the George H. W. Bush administration and later served as U.S. ambassador to NATO during the Clinton years. The undersecretary is the department's third-ranking official and its senior career diplomat. Burns served as the day-to-day manager of overall regional and bilateral policy issues, and he oversaw six geographically defined bureaus and two functional bureaus that reported to the undersecretary: bureaus for Africa, East Asia and the Pacific, Europe and Eurasia, the Near East, South Asia, the Western Hemisphere, International Organizations, and International Narcotics and Law Enforcement.

Another familiar face in the State Department would be Karen Hughes. Hughes, a former television news reporter, was George W. Bush's long-standing friend and advisor for more than 10 years, having served as his director of communications during Bush's six years as governor of Texas. Hughes was a counsel to the President during the first 18 months of his first administration and she was a communications consultant for Bush's second campaign. In her new role in the State Department, Hughes would serve as the undersecretary for public diplomacy and public affairs, which meant she would help ensure that public diplomacy was practiced in harmony with public affairs and traditional diplomacy to advance U.S. interests and security and to provide the moral basis for U.S. leadership in the world.

The undersecretary for economic, business, and agricultural affairs was Josette S. Shiner. Formerly an editor for *The Washington Times*, Shiner had extensive experience on the Council for Foreign Relations, as a deputy U.S. trade representative, and with William Bennett's group Empower America. As the undersecretary, Shiner would advise Rice on international economic policy.

Robert Joseph, formerly Rice's NSC staff assistant for nonproliferation, was named undersecretary for arms control and international security. The undersecretary leads the interagency policy process on nonproliferation and manages global U.S. security policy, principally in the areas of nonproliferation, arms control, regional security and defense relations, and arms transfers and security assistance.

The undersecretary for management was Henrietta H. Fore. The undersecretary for management leads the bureaus of administration, consular affairs, diplomatic security, human resources, information resource management, and overseas buildings operations, the Foreign Service Institute, the Office of Medical Services, the Office of Management Policy, the Office of Rightsizing the U.S. Government's Overseas Presence, and the White House liaison.

The undersecretary for democracy and global affairs was Paula J. Dobriansky. This undersecretary coordinates U.S. foreign relations on a variety of global issues, including democracy, human rights, and labor; environment, oceans, and science; narcotics control and law enforcement; population, refugees, and migration; and women's issues.

Among Rice's aides were other familiar names, including Jendayi Frazer, Rice's former graduate student. Frazer served as assistant secretary in the bureau for African affairs. Stephen Hadley, a former Vulcan and former principal of the Scowcroft Group, was named Rice's successor as national security advisor. He would continue to work closely with Rice and her department.

Rice's duties as secretary of state seem daunting at first glance (see Appendix 3 for a complete list). Among her key responsibilities is to serve as the president's principal advisor on U.S. foreign policy and to conduct negotiations relating to U.S. foreign affairs. She helps to advise the president on the appointment of U.S. ambassadors, ministers, consuls, and other diplomatic representatives, and she personally participates in or directs U.S. representatives to international conferences, organizations, and agencies. Rice also has the responsibility of negotiating, interpreting, and terminating treaties and agreements, and she must ensure the U.S. government's protection of American citizens and property, and American interests in foreign countries.

When Secretary of State Rice is not traveling around the world to meet with foreign diplomats and world leaders, she holds a half-hour meeting at 8 A.M. with members of her inner circle and a few other aides to plan her day. After this, on every Monday, Wednesday, and Friday she meets with her assistant secretaries and undersecretaries to hear reports on key events. On Tuesdays and Thursdays, she meets with her undersecretaries to plot strategies. Then, between 6:30 and 7:00 P.M., she again meets with members of her inner circle to review the day's events and plan the following day (Kessler, 2005, 7 June). World events unfold quickly, and it is important for the secretary of state and the undersecretaries to be in continual communication about what is transpiring and what the United States should be doing.

Rice does not like to use e-mail to communicate with her staff. Instead, she would rather hold a series of face-to-face meetings or phone conversations (Kessler, 2005, 7 June), and she is known to hold dinner meetings with key U.S. officials as well as her foreign counterparts. Rice often has working dinners that last for several hours to discuss difficult and complex issues of world security and foreign diplomacy.

MENDING FENCES

When Rice took office as secretary of state, there was much speculation and hope that she would take a very pragmatic view of foreign policy and attempt to work diplomatically to repair relationships between the United States and other parts of the world. Unlike her predecessor, Colin Powell, Rice became known for spending a great deal of her time traveling overseas, often making overnight trips in the cramped quarters of Air Force Two.

Her grueling schedule began in earnest on February 4, 2005, when Rice took her first trip abroad as secretary of state to mend fences and deliver tough messages concerning Iran. Iran has had long-standing human rights offenses, including executions of political activists without due process of law, arbitrary arrests and persecution of prisoners, deteriorating freedom of the press and freedom to assemble, and continued stoning of men and women convicted of adultery and homosexuality, even though judges were told at the end of 2002 to stop imposing this sentence. Furthermore, Iran's development of nuclear power was of significant concern to the international community. Germany, France, and Britain had negotiators working with Iran for several months to disclose the full extent of its nuclear program, but to little avail. Rice was clear that Iran's nuclear program needed to be halted or the country would face what she referred to as "the next steps." She continued by emphasizing the need for diplomacy:

The message that we are giving to Iran: We do have diplomatic means at our disposal, we are doing this bilaterally as well as multilaterally, and I believe that a diplomatic solution is in our grasp, if we can have unity of purpose, unity of message with the Iranians and if the Iranians understand that the international community is quite serious about it living up to its obligations. (Rice, as quoted in CNN, 2005)

It was a whirlwind trip as Rice visited eight countries in Europe as well as Israel and the Palestinian territories in the Middle East in just seven days. She made widely publicized stops in Germany, the United Kingdom, Poland, Turkey, Italy, France, Belgium, and Luxembourg. She met with Britain's Prime Minister Tony Blair, Germany's Chancellor Gerhard Schroeder, Palestinian President Mahmoud Abbas, Israeli Foreign Minister Silvan Shalom, Russian Foreign Minister Sergei Lavrov, Italian Prime Minister Gianfranco Fini, and a host of NATO and European Union (EU) officials.

Throughout her trip, Rice delivered the message that U.S.–European alliances needed to be restored. While in Paris, she made it very clear that the rift between the United and Europe over the Iraq war needed to be mended and a "new chapter" in American–European alliances had to be forged. French Ambassador Jean David Levitte observed that Rice "really changed the atmosphere—of the media, of public opinion—about the Bush administration. It was really a turning point." Based on her work during her first six months in office, Levitte concluded that Rice was "probably the most powerful secretary of state in decades" (Wright and Kessler, 2005). Egyptian Ambassador Nabil Fahmy seemed to agree. He noted, "The world's general reaction to her has been positive so far.... That's not to say we agree with everything she says or does, but that's not the criteria" (Wright and Kessler, 2005).

In her new role, Rice sought to forward a practical idealism—a political strategy that would bridge differences between the realist political theories of former Secretary of State Colin Powell and the neoconservative beliefs of Vice President Dick Cheney and others at the White House. The realists wanted to find common ground with allies around the world, while the neoconservatives felt that the United States was superior in the world and had the responsibility to remake other nations to become more aligned with its own morals and values, even if it meant disenfranchising America's long-standing allies. Rice adhered to the administration's belief that the United States held a superior position among the international community but she tried to work through diplomatic means rather than threats of armed engagements to maintain and develop that position.

THE ASIAN TOUR

In March, 2005, Rice embarked on an Asian tour, beginning with India. She began her talks with Indian Prime Minister Manmohan Singh, encouraging the leader to improve relations between India and Pakistan. The leaders also discussed the political situations in Nepal and Kashmir. After her meetings in India, Rice left New Delhi to visit the city of Islamabad in Pakistan. While in Islamabad, Rice discussed the support the country was giving to the U.S. war on terror.

Rice continued her tour with stops in Afghanistan, Japan, South Korea, and China. Her stop in China held particular significance because China posed threats to trade and the country was building its national defense. Both issues concerned the Bush administration, and Rice addressed these head-on in her meetings with Chinese officials. During her meetings, she emphasized the need for cooperation between China and the United States, particularly concerning the Six-Party Talks with North Korea to end the latter's development of nuclear weapons. Rice felt that China played a very key, and potentially powerful, role as China, Japan, the United States, Russia, North Korea, and South Korea worked to diplomatically resolve the issues North Korea's nuclear program presented. China seemed to have the closest relationship with North Korea of any country involved in the talks. In addition to sharing an 850-mile border, China had significant financial investments in North Korea.

Rice, who attended church services while in Beijing, also discussed human rights concerns with China, including freedom of religion and the extension of personal freedoms to the Chinese people. In a press conference, she explained:

Well, first of all, on human rights I made clear in raising a number of individual cases, as we always do, as well as some of the structural issues about human rights in China, that while we have seen some progress over the last few months that we expect that progress to continue, that the United States hopes that there will be improved relations in religious freedom with the Catholic Church, with the Dalai Lama's representatives, so that Tibetans can freely pursue their cultural interests. We also talked a good deal about the need for China to think about a more open political system that will match its economic openness and allow for the full creativity of the Chinese people … people must have an opportunity to exercise their religious beliefs, to exercise their religious traditions, to do so in an atmosphere that is free of intimidation, that in fact allows for the expansion of religion and communities of believers.... I do hope that there is an understanding that religious communities are not a threat to transitioning societies; in fact, they are very often in societies that are changing a force for good, for stability and for compassion in societies that are undergoing rapid change.... I think my commitment to religious freedom is well understood in this country and worldwide, and I said to Minister Li that, to my mind, this was not just something that I raise when I come to China or when he comes to the United States, but is something that we have to work on every day because I noted that the United States was, of course, founded by people who were fleeing religious persecution, many of them, and that this is a deeply held value for the United States of America, for the American people, and that it will continue to be a major issue in U.S.–China relations. (Rice, 2005)

Finally, Rice discussed concerns about Taiwan. Although the United States supported maintaining the status quo between China and Taiwan, the United States also had not ceased arms sales to the island. This presented more of a problem for China than it did for Taiwan, since Taiwan has arms support from the United States. However, there remained a great deal of tension between Taiwan and the mainland, and much concern about Taiwanese independence from China.

RUSSIA

In April, 2005, Rice met with Russia's President Vladimir Putin. As she made her way by plane to Russia, she conveyed messages critical of Putin to the reporters. She accused the leader of wielding too much power and not allowing more freedom for the Russian press. Before the meeting with Putin, Rice engaged in a radio interview, addressing callers' questions and encouraging strong ties between the two countries that were formerly Cold War enemies. When a caller asked Rice whether the United States's export of democracy was any different from the former Communist goals to export social revolution, she replied by asking whether people wanted to be "free from the knock of the secret police at night, people will say 'yes.' " She added that the United States would only speak out in favor of people's rights to have a say in their own futures, nothing more (MosNews, 2005a).

Later in her visit, as she met with President Putin, Rice encouraged him to consider the ways the former Soviet state could have stronger ties with the United States through trade and the war on terror. Rice emphasized the need for Russia to continue to develop its democracy, but she tempered her criticism of what many in the Bush administration felt was an eroding democracy in Russia. Some critics felt that the administration was treading too lightly with the Russian government so the two countries could remain allies. Even former Secretary of State Colin Powell pointedly noted the erosion of democracy in Russia while he was still in office. But Rice remained consistent with Bush and avoided such sharp criticism of the former Cold War rival. Instead, she suggested that the United States should open possibilities for Russia to join the World Trade Organization, and she noted that open markets encouraged open societies (MosNews, 2005b). Rice paved the way for President Bush to visit with President Putin the following month, as the two leaders joined more than 50 other world leaders in Moscow to commemorate the end of World War II.

During her visit, a young schoolgirl asked Rice if she planned to become president of the United States. Rice, who is fluent in Russian, at first responded "Da" (which means "Yes"). Then, when she realized her error, she quickly corrected herself by repeating "Nyet, nyet, nyet" ("No"). This error made news headlines around the world as people began to openly speculate about Rice's potential run for the presidency.

RETURN TO THE COMMONWEALTH CLUB

On May 27, 2005, Condoleezza Rice returned to the Commonwealth Club in San Francisco to deliver her first speech as secretary of state in this venue. Over 1,400 people gathered in Davies Symphony Hall to hear her speak. Rice did not seem to be deterred by the approximately 200 protestors gathered outside to voice opposition to Bush administration foreign policy. Likewise, she did not miss a beat when, five minutes into her talk, three protestors rose from their chairs in black robes and hoods reminiscent of the photos of prisoner abuse in Abu Ghraib. Abu Ghraib is an Iraqi city approximately 20 miles west of Baghdad. It first received notoriety as a place where Saddam Hussein tortured prisoners. Just before Rice's speech, news broke that the U.S. military also tortured prisoners at the same site. As the protestors chanted, "Stop the killing, stop the suicide, USA out of Iraq," Rice calmly observed how wonderful it was that in America people can speak their minds. The audience applauded to show support for Rice.

Throughout the speech, Rice kept her comments direct and clear. After noting how glad she was to be back in California and near Stanford University, Rice explained to the audience that President Bush believed "The best hope for peace in our world is the expansion of freedom in all the world." Then she explained her understanding of the administration's policies:

> Trying to label our policies as either realistic or idealistic is a false choice. It is both. Freedom and democracy are the only way for diverse societies to resolve their disputes justly and to live together without oppression and war. Our challenge today is to create conditions of openness around states that encourage and nurture democratic reform within states. America must open a path to the march of freedom across the entire world. We are succeeding in this great purpose, and we measure our success in the democratic revolutions that have stunned the entire world, vibrant revolutions of rose and orange and purple and tulip and cedar. (Rice, 2005)

She acknowledged that challenges for democracy and freedom still loomed large in the world, and she noted the need for changes in Latin America—changes she felt could be realized through the Central America Free Trade Agreement (CAFTA). She described the Millenium Challenge Account that would bring U.S. aid to the development of democratic institutions in Central America and Africa, provided the countries who applied for aid would follow the rules set forth by the U.S. government. As Rice noted the movement toward democracy throughout the world, particularly throughout Asia, she explained, "Democracy, a belief in liberty, a desire to be free, is as natural as breathing." She concluded that it was only through "keeping our faith with the highest ideals" that the United States would succeed in fostering human liberty throughout the world.

Perhaps one of the most challenging places Rice would encounter as she worked to realize this ideal was the Middle East. Not only was the situation in Iraq worsening as insurgents launched daily attacks against American and Iraqi troops and civilians, but also Israel and Palestine presented new challenges as the administration attempted to broker agreements to soothe the hostilities between these two disparate groups.

ISRAEL AND PALESTINE

Israeli Prime Minister Ariel Sharon ordered Israelis to withdraw from settlements in the Gaza Strip in August, 2005. From the time of the Six-Day War in the Middle East in 1967, Israel occupied Palestinian territory and the Gaza Strip and, after its withdrawal from the territory, Israel retained tight control of the crossing points. Since Israel and

Palestine were unable to reach agreement about this, the Gaza Strip remained largely sealed off, with neither people nor goods able to cross in and out of the area. This situation had the potential to devastate the region economically, essentially ruining chances for growth before the Palestinians had any real opportunity to develop the region.

Late on the evening of November 14, 2005, Rice led a vigorous diplomatic campaign to broker a deal between the Israelis and the Palestinians. At 11:00 P.M., Rice began to mediate one of her most significant series of meetings as secretary of state. From the ninth floor of the David Citadel Hotel in Jerusalem, she met alternatively with Israeli and Palestinian delegations and she did not allow either side to stop or to sleep until an agreement was reached. She worked through each item of concern brought to the table from each side, walking the corridor of the hotel to confer with aides.

Rice realized one of her greatest diplomatic accomplishments when, by midmorning on November 15, Israel and Palestine agreed to terms of operations that would allow Palestinians and their goods to cross between Gaza and the West Bank. The agreement included plans for a bus system and for the Palestinians to work on construction in Gaza's seaport and airport. While it was unclear when the renovations would be complete and these transportation centers would open, the plans were clearly a step forward. Rice explained,

> The important thing here is that people have understood that there is an important balance between security on the one hand and, on the other hand, allowing the Palestinian people freedom of movement.... The other important point is that everybody recognizes that if the Palestinians can move more freely and export their agriculture, that Gaza will be a much better place, where the institutions of democracy can begin to take hold. (Rice, as quoted in Wright and Wilson, 2005)

Rice and her tough diplomatic style were credited with this accomplishment. Yet, as violence again erupted between the two nations in early December, 2005, it remained clear that there was still much diplomatic work ahead to realize peace between these two groups.

HOMELAND

On August 29, 2005, Hurricane Katrina slammed the Gulf Coast of the United States, leaving over 1,000 people dead, more than 6,000 missing, and countless people displaced to other parts of the country. As levees broke in New Orleans and the historic city flooded, many Americans looked on in horror and disbelief. Was this really happening in the United States? Could an entire city, an entire region, be lost? As images of people stranded on rooftops and in the New Orleans Superdome reached the major news networks, tough questions were raised about the Bush administration's preparation for and response to the disaster.

As the news from New Orleans was unfolding, Condoleezza Rice was on vacation in New York City. On Wednesday evening, while 3,000 people were stranded at the New Orleans Convention Center with no food, water, or electricity, Rice attended the Broadway musical "Spamalot" in New York City. As the musical ended and the lights went up in the historic Shubert Theater, audience members booed the secretary of state. While visiting the city, she went shopping at Ferragamo, a trendy leather goods store on Fifth Avenue, reportedly purchasing several thousand dollars worth of shoes. When another shopper recognized Rice, the woman yelled at her, "How dare you shop for shoes when thousands are dying and homeless!" (Piazza and Rovzar, 2005). Rice also visited the U.S. Open and hit some tennis balls with Monica Seles before returning to Washington. Her staffers assured reporters that she was in appropriate contact with the State Department concerning events in areas hit by the hurricane.

On the evening of September 2, Rice issued a brief from the State Department to thank the international community for the response and support offered to the United States and the victims of Hurricane Katrina. At first, the administration refused to accept aid but, as the reports of the devastation worsened, aid was accepted from countries around the world, including Canada, the Netherlands, Russia, Israel, China, Italy, Turkey, the Phillipines, Azerbaijan, Australia, El Salvador, and even Sri Lanka, which was still recovering from the devastating tsunami that had hit the country just months before. As Rice explained the way the State Department was working to coordinate aid efforts from around the world, she added:

On a personal note, as you know, my family is from Alabama. My father was born and raised in Louisiana. The pictures are pictures that I, in many cases, know well. And I just want to say to the people of the hard-hit Gulf region that our prayers and thoughts, and my personal prayers and thoughts, are with them. I am going to travel this Sunday to Alabama to tour the disaster area, to meet with senior officials and Americans in need, and to receive briefings on the latest situation there. (Rice, 2005)

Yet, her personal condolences were not enough to stop harsh criticisms of the Bush administration's response to the crisis.

As could be expected, Rice came to President Bush's defense. While some felt that the lack of response from the federal government reflected racism in the United States, Rice vehemently responded that race had nothing to do with the government's response. As Rice visited her home state of Alabama, she told reporters:

I don't believe for a minute anybody allowed people to suffer because they are African-Americans. I just don't believe it for a minute…. Nobody, especially the president, would have left people unattended on the basis of race. (Daily, 2005)

While she denied that the response reflected racism in the United States, Rice acknowledged that the response could have been better:

People couldn't evacuate who were poor, people couldn't evacuate who were elderly, people couldn't evacuate who were sick. We have to understand better so this doesn't happen again. (Daily, 2005)

Rice's words fell short of explaining the Bush administration's decision to stop funding to the U.S. Army Corps of Engineers for the levee system in New Orleans, and she was not able to explain the wetland development that made the effects of the hurricane even more devastating (Blumenthal, 2005).

CANADA

Although Canada is the closest of any foreign country to Washington, D.C., Rice did not visit that nation until October 24, 2005. In her day and a half trip, she met with Prime Minister Paul Martin and Foreign Minister Pierre Pettigrew, as well as several Canadian parliamentarians. En route to Canada, Rice explained to the press the agenda for the meetings and the topics for discussion. The United States and Canada shared many international concerns, including relationships with Haiti and Sudan and the war on terror. Canada was considering a larger role in Afghanistan when NATO leadership changed in the year ahead. In addition, there were bilateral issues for the leaders to discuss, including NAFTA and the

North American Aerospace Defense Command (NORAD). This was no small agenda for discussions.

While in Canada, Susan Bonner of the Canadian Broadcasting Corporation interviewed Rice. Bonner first questioned Rice about why she visited 39 countries as secretary of state before traveling to Canada. Rice noted that she had had numerous conversations with Minister Pettigrew and that she had planned an earlier trip to Canada that had to be cancelled because of a scheduling problem. She assured radio listeners that she planned to make many trips to Canada in the future as she continued her duties as secretary of state. Bonner and Rice continued the interview by discussing a number of issues of concern to Canadians that differed, in part, from Rice's stated agenda when she traveled to the country: softwood lumber, trade disputes, requiring passports to travel across the border between the two countries, gun control, and the roles of Canada and the United States in Afghanistan and Iraq.

Rice's visit had a mixed reception among the Canadian population. John McNamer, an American who was a decorated Vietnam War veteran turned peace activist and had emigrated to Canada with his family in 1987, petitioned Prime Minister Paul Martin to not allow Rice into the country because of alleged U.S. violations of the Geneva Convention. Protests were planned in Halifax and other cities, and the Maritimes Independent Media Centre issued a call for people to participate in the protest, announcing that "Canadians will not welcome a war criminal!" The group held a public vigil for victims of U.S. occupations and Canada's complicity in illegal wars of aggression. The group also aired the documentary *The Oil Factor*, which exposed connections between the Bush administration's roles in the oil industry and war.

Rice held firm to the administration's goals throughout her visit. She did not waiver on the issue of whether the United States should repay $4 billion it collected illegally in excess trade tariffs on Canadian softwood lumber, and she expressed her displeasure with Canada's withdrawal from the U.S. missile defense program. Her visit seemed to do little to change the souring relationship between the two governments. Instead, it seemed to remind Canadians of their irritation with the U.S. government and American citizens, which was reported to be more unfavorable than ever; some speculated that the relationship between the two countries would not be repaired until the Bush administration was no longer in office (Struck, 2005).

HOMECOMING

In October, 2005, Rice had a widely publicized homecoming to Alabama. Traveling with British Foreign Secretary Jack Straw and British Ambassador David Manning, she visited several places that were central to her childhood. She stopped by the Brunetta C. Hill Elementary School that she attended as a young girl, visiting with children and answering their questions in the library. She spoke at a ceremony honoring her friend Denise McNair and the other three girls who were killed in the 16th Street Baptist Church bombing in 1963. She traveled to Tuscaloosa to the Bryant-Denny Stadium to see the University of Alabama football team defeat their rival, Tennessee.

A secretary of state does not typically engage in domestic travels or concerns, so it was unusual to see Rice traveling to Alabama rather than to Seoul or some other foreign capital. However, the purpose of the trip was connected to foreign concerns, at least in principle. The Bush administration hoped that Rice would draw parallels between what happened in her childhood in Birmingham and the administration's broader efforts to build democracy abroad.

> Not only is Birmingham my home, but Birmingham is evocative of the, I'll use the word terror, that also attended ... the depths of Jim Crow," she told reporters on the flight to Alabama. The history of how African Americans won civil rights, she said, illustrates "that the United States should have a certain humility when it talks about the spread of democracy and liberty but also that freedom denied is not always denied, that, in fact, there comes a time when people are able to rise up and to get their freedom." (Rice, as quoted in Robinson, 2005a)

Although some critics may have thought that her comparison was a bit of a stretch, the people of Alabama seemed to be really proud of her and glad that she visited the city that once was her home.

On October 30, 2005, Rice attended a memorial service in Montgomery for civil rights activist Rosa Parks, who had died just a few days before. Rice said of Parks:

> I'll always remember her as a quiet and dignified woman, but also as a symbol of how individuals make a difference. And we tend to

think sometimes of the great sweep of history, the great movements of history, but very often it's an individual that inspires people, and she inspired a lot of people. (Rice, in an interview with Bonner, 2005)

However, the differences between these two influential women were certainly easier to notice than the similarities. While both were from Alabama, they represented different social classes and different aims. Parks stood with the oppressed, while Rice stood with the oppressors (Richmond, 2005).

As Rice attended the memorial service for Parks in Montgomery, she was seated beside Reverend Joseph Lowery, a long-time civil rights leader and founder of the Southern Christian Leadership Conference (SCLC). Lowery pleaded with Rice, "Dr. Rice, Sister Secretary of State, what a glorious tribute it would be if you and the governor of Alabama and the mayor of Montgomery would join John Conyers and Sister Kilpatrick and John Lewis in extending the Voting Rights Act" (Democracy Now, 2003). He was one of many in the African American community who hoped Rice would turn her attention toward the plight of African Americans in the United States (Robinson, 2005b).

IRAQ

On Veteran's Day, November 11, 2005, Rice made her second visit to Iraq as secretary of state. It was a surprise visit, conducted with much secrecy and heavy security. Rice entered Baghdad by helicopter because it was too dangerous for her to arrive by car from the airport—the road was notorious for insurgent attacks. Rice stressed that success in Iraq was in the best interests of everyone and, after a meeting with local officials, she stated, "If Iraq does not succeed, and if Iraq becomes a place of despair, generations of Americans would also be condemned to fear."

While Rice was visiting with soldiers in Iraq, President Bush was speaking to troops at an Army depot in Tobyhanna, Pennsylvania. He told the soldiers and their families that those who were criticizing the war were "deeply irresponsible ... the stakes in the global war on terror are too high, and the national interest is too important, for politicians to throw out false charges. These baseless attacks send the wrong signal to our troops and to an enemy that is questioning America's will" (Stevenson, 2005).

Questions about the war in Iraq would plague Rice throughout her first year as secretary of state. As the Iraqi elections took place in December, it seemed that this could mark a level of accomplishment in the war. However, controversy continued as *The New York Times* printed a story about the Bush administration ordering the National Security Agency to secretly spy on American citizens without the necessary judicial approval. Rice came to the administration's defense once again, sharing the president's claim that secret wiretapping was necessary to protect the United States during the war on terror. However, there were some who pointed out that this was a crime that would be impeachable. Both Republican and Democratic senators called for an investigation into this matter.

LOYALTY TO THE PRESIDENT

While Rice's intelligence and hard work were widely acknowledged and admired traits, the characteristic that defined Rice more than any other was her loyalty to President Bush. She spent a great deal of time covering for him and smoothing over errors committed by his administration (Reid, 2005). Perhaps most notable was in April, 2005, when *The Washington Post* reported that Rice's State Department would not make public in its annual report to Congress the fact that international terrorist incidents had more than tripled since 2003 (Glasser, 2005). The report is mandated by law [Title 22 of U.S. Code, Section 2656f(a)] and requires that a full and complete report on terrorism be submitted to Congress by April 30 of each year (Wendland, 2005).

In the 2005 report, terrorist incidents were numbered at 655 significant attacks. To be considered a significant attack, civilians must have been killed. This figure did not include attacks on the military in Iraq or Afghanistan. The number in the 2005 report included violence in India's Kashmir territory, attacks on trains in Madrid, ongoing violence in Israel, and Chechen rebels attacks on school children in Belsan, Russia. Furthermore, the State Department would not indicate how many people had been killed worldwide in terrorist attacks.

Critics felt Rice's withholding of the report was an attempt to shield the government from criticism that the war on terror was not working and that the U.S. military presence in Afghanistan and Iraq was only intensifying terrorist efforts. People who supported Bush claimed that Rice was just waiting to get more accurate numbers (Wendland, 2005). Republican and Democratic aides alike insisted that it was "absurd" for the State Department to claim that the statistics were not relevant to the required report on global terrorism trends. Yet, Karen Aguila, the State Department's acting counterterrorism chief, reported that advice to Rice to withhold these statistics came from her counselor, Philip Zelikow, Rice's former colleague and executive director of the 9/11 Commission (Glasser, 2005).

RETURN TO EUROPE

As Rice's first year as secretary of state came to a close, she returned to Europe, visiting some countries she went to during her first trip abroad as secretary of state. During the first week of December, 2005, Rice embarked on a trip to Germany, Belgium, Ukraine, and Romania. She fielded tough questions about the rumors of U.S./CIA-run prisons in Europe holding suspected terrorists, explaining that the United States sometimes deports suspected terrorists to third-party countries for questioning, but never uses torture. She explained, "The United States government does not authorize or condone torture of detainees. Torture and conspiracy to commit torture are crimes under U.S. law, wherever they may occur in the world" (Stroebel, 2005). While in Berlin, Rice admitted that the United States might make mistakes in its war on terrorism, and she promised to put them right if they happened. She explained, "We recognize [that] any policy will sometimes result in errors, and when it happens, we will do everything we can to rectify it" (Hudson and Charbonneau, 2005). Leaders throughout Europe expressed satisfaction with Rice's assurances, while many European people and media remained skeptical of her comments (Bernstein, 2005).

FUTURE PRESIDENT?

At the end of her first year as secretary of state, Rice held higher public opinion ratings than any other top administration official. At a time when the president's and vice president's approval ratings had plummeted to 30 percent or 40 percent, a USA Today/CNN/Gallup poll showed Rice with approval ratings at 63 percent (Slavin, 2005). She was considered by many to be the Republican Party's best chance to retain the White House in the 2008 elections. Web sites devoted to supporting her campaign for U.S. president sprung up with sponsorship from the sale of bumper stickers and bobble-head dolls. Political consultant Dick Morris coauthored with Eileen McGann a widely sold book *Condi vs. Hillary: The Next Great Presidential Debate* to speculate about what this competition might bring, and he advocated for her to run for office.

In October, 2005, there were rumors circulating throughout Washington and the world that Vice President Cheney would resign in the midst of the Valerie Plame scandal and that Bush would appoint Rice as vice president. On October 16, 2005, Rice insisted on NBC's *Meet the Press* that she would not run for President in 2008. This was a message she continued when Susan Bonner of the Canadian Broadcasting Corporation questioned Rice about a possible run for the presidency:

I never ran for anything, not even for high school president. No, I know my place and we have an exceptional opportunity now in these exceptional days to try and, through our shared values with places like Canada and Great Britain and other countries, to help others who have been denied liberty and freedom to find that liberty and freedom, and that's what I'd like to devote my energies to. (Rice, 2005)

Rice did not seem to become distracted by those who questioned whether she would run for the presidency, and she expressed confidence that some day an African American woman would win the presidency. However, at least for the moment, it did not seem to be her dream.

Secretaries of State Who Later Served as U.S. President

Thomas Jefferson (served under George Washington)

James Madison (served under Thomas Jefferson)

John Quincy Adams (served under James Monroe)

Martin van Buren (served under Andrew Jackson)

James Buchanan (served under James Polk)

Throughout her first year as secretary of state, Rice remained poised, confident, and articulate. She faced tough questioning and difficult challenges that would test her abilities and carry profound consequences for people and governments throughout the world. In response to a young child's questions when she visited her former elementary school in Birmingham, Rice admitted, "It's not easy being secretary of state ... but it's fun" (Robinson, 2005a). Few people could know this. She had certainly accomplished what many others could not, and she continued to give tribute to her parents and others who helped to pave the way for her:

I think back to my mom and dad, who gave me every opportunity. It didn't matter what I wanted to learn, they tried to provide the opportunity to do it. And I think back to the multitude of teachers in segregated Birmingham who took money out of their own pockets to buy textbooks for kids when there weren't free textbooks for black kids. And I think that this is not what I've achieved. This is what a whole generation, indeed generations, of people in places like segregated Alabama achieved, the struggles and the sacrifice.... It's still a struggle for many. But, it's not my achievement. It's the achievement of generations. (Fox News, 2005, 30 January)

Appendix 1

GEORGE W. BUSH CABINET

Office	Name	Term
President	George W. Bush	2001–
Vice President	Richard B. Cheney	2001–
State	Colin L. Powell	2001–2005
	Condoleezza Rice	2005–
Defense	Donald H. Rumsfeld	2001–
Treasury	Paul H. O'Neill	2001–2003
	John W. Snow	2003–
Justice	John D. Ashcroft	2001–2005
	Alberto R. Gonzales	2005–
Interior	Gale A. Norton	2001–
Agriculture	Ann M. Veneman	2001–2005
	Mike Johanns	2005–
Commerce	Donald L. Evans	2001–2005
	Carlos M. Gutierrez	2005–
Labor	Elaine L. Chao	2001–
Health and Human Services	Tommy G. Thompson	2001–2005
	Michael O. Leavitt	2005–

Housing and Urban Development	Melquiades R. Martinez	2001–2003
	Alphonso R. Jackson	2004–
Transportation	Norman Y. Mineta	2001–
Energy	E. Spencer Abraham	2001–2005
	Samuel W. Bodman	2005–
Education	Roderick R. Paige	2001–2005
	Margaret Spellings	2005–
Veterans Affairs	Anthony J. Principi	2001–2005
	James Nicholson	2005–
Homeland Security	Thomas J. Ridge	2003–2005
	Michael Chertoff	2005–

(Information in this appendix is from Wikipedia, George W. Bush cabinet. http://en.wikipedia.org/wiki/George_W_Bush)

Appendix 2

PROTEST STATEMENT DISTRIBUTED AT 2002 STANFORD GRADUATION

COMMENCEMENT WITH CONDOLEEZZA RICE

This document was distributed at the 2002 Stanford Commencement Ceremonies by a student group called the Redwood Action Team. The full document can be found at http://www.stanford.edu/group/rats/condi.

At this year's graduation ceremony, a number of Stanford students and community members will be engaging in a non-disruptive protest of the actions taken by Condoleezza Rice in her roles as National Security Advisor, Stanford Provost, and member of the Chevron Board of Directors.

If you would like to send Dr. Rice a message of protest, we encourage you to do the following as she begins speaking:

STUDENTS, FACULTY AND STAFF: Fold this flyer to fit your mortarboard and attach it using the three paperclips. When Dr. Rice begins speaking, hold up your cap (with the flyer) towards her and continue holding it for as long as you feel comfortable.

FAMILY MEMBERS AND GUESTS: When Dr. Rice begins speaking, please hold up your flyers.

The following is a partial list of actions taken and policies advocated by Condoleezza Rice. The consequences of these actions and policies are a source of great concern to the hundreds of students and Stanford community members who have signed a petition objecting to them, and to those of us taking part in today's protest:

National Security Advisor: As national security advisor to the Bush administration, Dr. Rice has:

1. Called for the US to remove itself from the following international agreements,:

   - The Comprehensive Test Ban Treaty
   - The Anti-Ballistic Missile Treaty
   - The International Criminal Court
   - The Kyoto Protocol

This strategy isolates the US from the global community and obstructs solutions to global problems, such as nuclear proliferation and global warming.

2. Advocated for the following policies in the wake of 9/11:

   - Unprecedented restriction of media coverage of the war in Afghanistan.
   - Increased polarization of the global communities following Bush's "with or against the US" ultimatum and his labeling of Iran, Iraq and North Korea as "The Axis of Evil."
   - An upgrading of Plan Colombia from a multi-billion dollar part of the "war on drugs" to an official part of the "War on Terrorism." This upgrade entails an increase in funding for the Colombian military, an organization that has consistently engaged in egregious human rights violations.
   - The development of smaller nuclear weapons for battlefield use and the creation of a nuclear hit list, a policy that undermines the fundamentals of nuclear deterrence.

Stanford Provost: While Provost at Stanford University (1993–1999), Condoleezza Rice took a number of actions that alienated various members of the Stanford community:

1. Defended Stanford's hiring and tenure processes while fielding a formally filed complaint from 15 female professors documenting discriminatory practices.
2. Denied departmental status to the African & African American Studies Program, and other emerging ethnic studies programs.
3. Refused to address the University's failure to find a director for the Stanford Center for Chicano Research.
4. Failed to honor the agreement negotiated with MEChA (Movimiento Estudiantil Chicano de Aztlán) hunger strikers.
5. Recommended consolidating all ethnic community centers from their current locations into a single building.

6. Weakened the Student Workshops on Political and Social Issues (SWOPSI) program which had supported dozens of student initiated courses.

7. Overturned a 1969 vote by the Academic Senate that had ended ROTC use of Stanford facilities.

Chevron Board Member: In the 10 years that Condoleezza Rice sat on the Chevron Board of Directors (1991–2001) she failed to respond to the numerous environmental and human rights abuses that the company was committing, even as chair of Chevron's Public Policy Committee (1999–2001), whose stated purpose was to "identify, monitor and evaluate domestic and foreign social, political and environmental issues" and "recommend to the board policies and strategies concerning such issues. These abuses occurred in places such as:

1. **Nigeria:** Since the early 1990s the Niger Delta region has been in a state of civil unrest as residents protest the destruction of their land by Chevron's operations in the area. Chevron was brought to US federal court in May 1999 for conspiring in the Nigerian military's campaign of execution, torture and cruel, inhuman and degrading treatment of these peaceful protestors. This includes the destruction of two villages by soldiers in Chevron helicopters and boats.

2. **Richmond, California:** Between 1991 and 1995, Chevron was accused of violating the federal Clean Water Act by bypassing its refinery's treatment system and discharging waste water that exceeded toxicity limits into San Francisco Bay.

3. **Southern California:** In March of 1991 a Chevron-chartered oil tanker ripped open undersea pipeline running to one of Chevron's refineries, and more than 27,000 gallons of oil spilled into Santa Monica Bay. In 1994, Chevron was fined for discharging untreated industrial waste into municipal sewers in the same area.

Appendix 3

DUTIES OF THE SECRETARY OF STATE

The information in this appendix is from the U.S. Department of State, http://www.state.gov.

FACT SHEET
Bureau of Public Affairs
Washington, DC
January 22, 2001

Under the Constitution, the President of the United States determines U.S. foreign policy. The Secretary of State, appointed by the President with the advice and consent of the Senate, is the President's chief foreign affairs adviser. The Secretary carries out the President's foreign policies through the State Department and the Foreign Service of the United States.

Created in 1789 by the Congress as the successor to the Department of Foreign Affairs, the Department of State is the senior executive Department of the U.S. Government. The Secretary of State's duties relating to foreign affairs have not changed significantly since then, but they have become far more complex as international commitments multiplied. These duties—the activities and responsibilities of the State Department—include the following:

- Serves as the President's principal adviser on U.S. foreign policy;
- Conducts negotiations relating to U.S. foreign affairs;
- Grants and issues passports to American citizens and exequaturs to foreign consuls in the United States;

- Advises the President on the appointment of U.S. ambassadors, ministers, consuls, and other diplomatic representatives;
- Advises the President regarding the acceptance, recall, and dismissal of the representatives of foreign governments;
- Personally participates in or directs U.S. representatives to international conferences, organizations, and agencies;
- Negotiates, interprets, and terminates treaties and agreements;
- Ensures the protection of the U.S. Government to American citizens, property, and interests in foreign countries;
- Supervises the administration of U.S. immigration laws abroad;
- Provides information to American citizens regarding the political, economic, social, cultural, and humanitarian conditions in foreign countries;
- Informs the Congress and American citizens on the conduct of U.S. foreign relations;
- Promotes beneficial economic intercourse between the United States and other countries;
- Administers the Department of State;
- Supervises the Foreign Service of the United States.

In addition, the Secretary of State retains domestic responsibilities that Congress entrusted to the State Department in 1789. These include the custody of the Great Seal of the United States, the preparation of certain presidential proclamations, the publication of treaties and international acts as well as the official record of the foreign relations of the United States, and the custody of certain original treaties and international agreements. The Secretary also serves as the channel of communication between the Federal Government and the States on the extradition of fugitives to or from foreign countries.

GLOSSARY

Bush Doctrine: a guiding principle of preemptive action President George W. Bush explained to the American public on the evening of September 11, 2001: "[G]o after the terrorists and those who harbor them."

chamber music: a form of classical music performed by a small group of musicians.

civil rights movement: in the United States, throughout the 1950s and 1960s there was a series of protests and efforts to ensure that all citizens had equal protection under the law, including the right to vote, the right to personal freedom, the right to life, the right to freedom of movement, and antidiscrimination. Positive liberty was a key ideal—the notion that people have the right to fulfill their own potential.

Cold War: the struggle between the United States and its allies and the Soviet Union and its allies that ensued after World War II until the fall of the Soviet Union in 1991. While there was no direct armed conflict, there were economic pressure, propaganda, and other strategic maneuvers to create an atmosphere of fear and threat of war.

communism: a system of government and a political theory based on common ownership of the means of production and a classless society.

con dolcezza: Italian musical phrase meaning "with sweetness" that was the inspiration for Condoleezza Rice's name.

conservatism: a political philosophy that supports traditional values and the established social order.

democracy: a system of government grounded in the ideal that people should participate in decisions about their own governance.

Iron Curtain: the symbolic, ideological, and physical boundary that separated Europe after World War II. Those countries in Eastern and Central Europe, the Eastern Bloc, were under the political influence of the Soviet Union and ruled by pro-Soviet governments. These countries included Bulgaria, Czechoslovakia, East Germany, Hungary, Poland, Romania, and Albania (until the early 1960s).

Jim Crow laws: codification of various aspects of American public life to separate whites from African Americans that were established and enforced in the early to mid-1900s.

Ku Klux Klan: a white supremacist group founded in 1865 in Pulaski, Tennessee. The group often resorted to violence to achieve its aims.

Kyoto Protocol: an international protocol on climate change that sought to limit the emission of carbon dioxide and other greenhouse gases that were believed to contribute to global warming. Drafted in 1997, 156 countries have ratified the agreement. Two notable exceptions are the United States and Australia.

liberal: a political ideology that seeks to maximize liberty for individuals and society, including fundamental rights to life, liberty, and property.

NAFTA: the North American Free Trade Agreement, which links the United States, Canada, and Mexico in a free trade sphere. The policy went into effect on January 1, 1994 with the intent of eliminating tariffs on imports and exports over a 14-year period.

NATO: the North Atlantic Treaty Organization is an international organization for defense alliance signed in 1949. With its headquarters in Belgium, NATO includes the following member states: Belgium, Bulgaria, Canada, Czech Republic, Denmark, Estonia, France, Germany, Greece, Hungary, Iceland, Italy, Latvia, Lithuania, Luxembourg, Netherlands, Norway, Poland, Portugal, Romania, Slovakia, Slovenia, Spain, Turkey, United Kingdom, and the United States.

neoconservatism: a political ideology characterized by interventionist views on foreign policy and a commitment to Judeo-Christian moral principles.

NORAD: the North American Aerospace Defense Command, operated jointly with Canada to provide aerospace warning and control for North America. Since 1963, the organization's main facility has been in Cheyenne Mountain, Colorado.

political moralism: a political philosophy grounded in the ideal that particular universal values need to be supported by everyone, including freedom and democracy.

political realism: a political philosophy grounded in the ideal that countries should be dealt with on their own terms. Countries should not try to change the governing structures of other countries.

Powell Doctrine: a set of principles to guide military policy during war that was developed by Colin Powell during the buildup to the first Gulf War in 1990 and 1991. Powell believed the military should employ full force and a quick exit strategy.

practical idealism: a political strategy Rice employed to bridge differences between political realists and neoconservatives. This strategy held firm to the moralistic beliefs that the United States held a superior position in relation to the rest of the international community, but it shifted away from threats of armed engagements to more diplomatic strategies.

Rice Doctrine: a set of principles to guide foreign policy so that the world was not just safer but better (Preble, 2005).

Sinatra Doctrine: Soviet leader Mikhail Gorbachev's loosening of Soviet restrictions on the internal affairs of Warsaw Pact countries, including Czechoslovakia, Poland, Bulgaria, Romania, Hungary, and East Germany.

Solidarity: a Polish national trade union led by shipyard electrician Lech Walesa. The group led a series of nonviolent protests in Poland in the 1980s that contributed to the end of communism in the country and served as a model of peaceful anticommunist counterrevolution in the Soviet Union and Eastern Europe.

Vulcans: an advisory team to George W. Bush when he campaigned for his first term as U.S. president. Members included Condoleezza Rice, Paul Wolfowitz, Richard Perle, Richard Armitage, Dov Zakheim, Stephen Hadley, Robert Blackwill, and Robert Zoellick. Many members of this team would go on to serve in various capacities in the first and second terms of the Bush administration.

REFERENCES

Acosta, A. (1998). Deep in the heart of Texas: The final four delivers serious hoops—and partying. *Stanford Magazine*. Available at http://www.stanfordalumni.org/news/magazine/1998/mayjun/articles/season_to_shout/heart_of_texas_sidebar.html.

Adelman. (2005). Dr. Adelman's research. Available at http://www.du.edu/gsis/faculty/adelman.html.

Alabama Slavery Code. (2005). Slave laws relating to speech and assembly. Available at http://www.wfu.edu/~zulick/340/slavecodes.html.

Associated Press (2000, 17 December). Exceeding expectations, Rice returns to White House in top job. Available at http://archives.cnn.com/2000/ALLPOLITICS/stories/12/17/rice.profile.ap/.

Bernstein, R. (2005, 11 December). News analysis: In Europe, two views of Rice's mission. Available at http://www.iht.com/articles/2005/12/11/news/assess.php.

The Black Commentator. (2003). Commentary. Available at www.blackcommentator.com/26/26_commentary.html.

Blumenthal, S. (2005, 2 September). Katrina comes home to roost. Available at http://www.guardian.co.uk/katrina/story/0,16441,1561356,00.html.

Brintzman, D. (2003). *Practice makes practices: A critical study of learning to teach*. Albany, NY: State University of New York Press.

Bush, G. W. (2002). *State of the Union*. Available at http://www.whitehouse.gov/news/releases/2002/01/20020129-11.html.

CNN. (2002, 8 September). Top Bush officials push case against Saddam. Available at http://archives.cnn.com/2002/ALLPOLITICS/09/08/iraq.debate.

CNN (2005, 9 February). Rice: Iran must halt nuclear program. Available at http://www.cnn.com/2005/WORLD/europe/02/09/rice/.

Cozzens, L. (1999). Freedom rides. Available at http://www.watson.org/~lisa/blackhistory/civilrights-55-65/freeride.html.

Cunningham, K. (2005). *Condoleezza Rice: U.S. secretary of state.* Chanhassen, MN: The Child's World.

Daily, M. (2005, 5 September). Rice denies race affected relief: Government can learn, improve its response, she says. Available at http://www.chron.com/cs/CDA/ssistory.mpl/nation/3339560.

Dallin, A., & Rice, C. (1986). *The Gorbachev era.* Stanford, CA: Stanford Alumni Association.

Davis, R.L.F. (n.d.) Creating Jim Crow: In-depth essay. Available at http://www.jimcrowhistory.org/history/creating2.htm.

Democracy Now. (2003). Joseph Lowery calls on Condoleezza Rice to extend Voting Rights Act. Available at http://www.democracynow.org/article.pl?sid = 05/11/03/1545240.

Ditchfield, C. (2003). *Condoleezza Rice: National security advisor.* New York: Scholastic.

Dowd, A. (2005, September & October). What makes Condi run. Available at http://www.aarpmagazine.org/people/condoleezza.html.

Du Bois, W.E.B. (1903/1989). *Souls of black folks.* New York: Penguin Books.

Eichler, T. (2001). Rumsfeld, Rice say U.S. will cooperate with others on missile defense. Available at http://www.fas.org/news/usa/2001/usa-010506.htm.

Evans, H. (1998). End of the cold war: America's turn to the right 1980–1989. Available at http://www.randomhouse.com/features/americancentury/totheright.html.

Felix, A. (2002). *Condi: The Condoleezza Rice story.* New York: Simon & Schuster.

Fox News (2005, 30 January). Condoleezza Rice interview with Chris Wallace. Available at http://www.newshounds.us/2005/01/30/fox_news_sunday_condoleezza_rice_interview.php.

Gee, J. (2001). What is literacy. In P. Shannon (Ed). *Becoming political, too.* (p. 1–9). Portsmouth, NH: Heinemann.

Gilbert, A. (2002). Condoleezza Rice and the president have lost their way. Available at http://www.commondreams.org/cgi-bin/print.cgi?file=/views02/1022–07.htm.

Glasser, S. (2005, 27 April). U.S. figures show sharp global rise in terrorism: State department will not put data in report. Available at http://www.washingtonpost.com/wp-dyn/content/article/2005/04/26/AR2005042601623_pf.html.

Gonzalez, A. (2004, 30 March). Letter from White House counsel. Available at http://news.findlaw.com/hdocs/docs/whouse/wh911c33004ltr2.html.

Griffin, D. (2004) *The 9/11 Commission report: Omissions and distortions.* New York: Olive Branch Press.

Grossman, K., & Long, J. (2001, 29 January). Star wars booster. Available at http://www.thenation.com/doc.mhtml?i=200110129&s=grossman.

GWU. (2005). Interview with Dr. Condoleezza Rice. Available at http://www.gwu.edu/~nsarchiv/coldwar/interviews/episode-24/rice3.html.

Haskins, J. (1995). *Freedom rides: Journey for justice.* New York: Hyperion.

Hudson, S., & Charbonneau, L. (2005, 6 December). US may make mistakes in 'war on terror': Rice. Available at http://today.reuters.com/News/newsArticle.aspx?type = topNews&storyID = 2005–12–06T114600Z_01_KRA637460_RTRUKOC_0_US-EUROPE-RICE-GERMANY.xml.

Hudson, S., & Mohammed, A. (2005, 19 January). Rice on defensive over Iraq, integrity. *Associated Press.* Available at http://ir.news.yahoo.com/050119/137/2j3pa.html.

Joffe, J. (1996). Putting Germany back together: The fabulous Bush and Baker boys. Available at http://www.foreignaffairs.org/19960101fareviewessay4180/josef-joffe/putting-germany-back-together-the-fabulous-bush-and-baker-boys.html.

Jones, C. (1986). The Soviet Union and the Czechoslovak army 1948–1983: Uncertain allegiance (Review). *Soviet Studies, 38 (4),* 602–604.

Journal of Blacks in Higher Education (2001). Among black scholars Condoleezza Rice leads the media citation count. *Journal of Blacks in Higher Education, 31,* 47–48.

Journal of Blacks in Higher Education (2005). History's milestones of African American higher education. *Journal of Blacks in Higher Education, 7,* 86–90.

Kaldova, Joseph. (2004). Czech mate for Condi. A review of Rice's *Uncertain Alliances.* Available at http://counterpunch.org/kalvoda04202004.html.

Kaplan, G. (2001). Transcript: national security adviser Dr. Condoleezza Rice. Available at http://www.wnyc.org/legacy/shows/madaboutmusic/madabout_transcript090701.html.

Kessler, G. (2005, 7 June). Rice taps longtime colleagues for inner circle. Available at http://www.washingtonpost.com/wp-dyn/content/article/2005/06/06/AR2005060601965.html.

Kessler, G. (2005, 17 January). Rice goes from the inside to the front. Available at http://www.washingtonpost.com/wp-dyn/articles/A14268–2005Jan16.html.

Kessler, G. (2004, 20 October). Rice hitting the road to speak. Available at http://www.washingtonpost.com/wp-dyn/articles/A46231–2004Oct19.html.

Kessler, G. (2004, 16 October). Scowcroft is critical of Bush. http://www.washingtonpost.com/wp-dyn/articles/A36644–2004Oct15.html.

Kettmann, S. (2000, 20 March). Bush's secret weapon. Available at http://www.salon.com/politics2000/feature/2000/03/20/rice/.

King Jr., M. L. (1963/1994). *Letters from a Birmingham jail*. New York: Harper Collins.

Kramer, M. (1985). Poland's politicized army: Communists in uniform; the Soviet Union and the Czechoslovak army, 1948–1983: Uncertain allegiance (Review). *International Affairs (Royal Institute of International Affairs 1994–)*, *61 (3)*, 527–529.

Lemann, N. (2002, 14 & 21 October). Without a doubt: Has Condoleezza Rice changed George W. Bush, or has he changed her? Available at http://www.newyorker.com/fact/content/articles/021014fa_fact3.

Mann, J. (2004). *Rise of the Vulcans: The history of Bush's war cabinet*. New York: Viking Press.

Marinucci, C. (2001, 5 May). Chevron redubs ship named for bus aide Condoleezza Rice drew too much attention. Available at http://www.sfgate.com/cgi-bin/article.cgi?file = /c/a/2001/05/05/MN223743.DTL.

Markovits, A. (1996). Germany unified and Europe transformed: A study in statecraft. [Review] *The American Political Science Review, 90 (3)*,712–713.

McKay, Claude. (1919). If we must die. Available at Poets' Corner, http://www.theotherpages.org/poems/mckay03.html.

McManamon, P. (2004, 14 October). Condoleezza Rice visits practice. Available at http://www.clevelandbrowns.com/news_room/news/arts/3297.0.html.

Miller, H. (1996). Germany unified and Europe transformed. *The Historical Journal, 39 (4)*, 1138–1140.

Morris, D., & McGann, E. (2005). *Condi vs. Hillary: The next great presidential debate*. New York: Regan Books.

MosNews (2005a, 20 April). Condoleezza Rice answers radio listeners' questions ahead of Putin meeting. Available at http://www.mosnews.com/news/2005/04/20/riceekho.shtml.

MosNews (2005b, 18 April). Rice seeks happy medium between democracy, terror war with Russia. Available at http://www.mosnews.com/news/2005/04/18/ricerussia.shtml.

MSNBC and NBC News (2004, 8 April). Rice defends anti-terror moves before 9/11. Available at http://www.msnbc.msn.com/id/4693043/.

National Security Archive (1997, 17 December). Interview with Condoleezza Rice. Available at http://www.gwu.edu/~nsarchiv/coldwar/interviews/episode-24/rice4.html.

New York Public Radio. (2005). Mad about music. Available at http://www.wnyc.org/shows/mam/episodes/2005/01/02.

NewsHour (1996, 4 July). What's next? Available at http://www.pbs.org/newshour/bb/europe/july96/runoff_results3_7–4.html.

NewsHour. (2004). Newsmaker: Condoleezza Rice. Available at http://www.pbs. org/newshour/bb/terrorism/july-dec04/rice_7-22.html.

Piazza, J., & Rovzar, C. (2005, 2 September). As south drowns, Rice soaks in N.Y. Available at http://www.nydailynews.com/news/gossip/story/ 342707p-292600c.html.

Plotz, D. (2000, 12 May). Condoleezza Rice: George W. Bush's celebrity advisor. Available at http://slate.msn.com/id/82463/.

Prados, J. (2004). Blindsided or blind? Highly qualified but strangely inattentive, Condoleezza Rice has missed the signs of the Soviet collapse, the importance of terrorism before 9/11, and more. *Bulletin of the Atomic Scientists, 60 (4)*, 27–37.

Preble, C. (2005, February). The Rice doctrine. *Foreign Service Journal*, 45–49.

Ransby, B. (2003). *Ella Baker and the black freedom movement: A radical democratic vision*. Chapel Hill: The University of North Carolina Press.

Ratnesar, R. (1999, 20 September). Condi Rice can't lose. Available at http:// www.cnn.com/ALLPOLITICS/time/1999/09/20/rice.html.

Redwood Action Team at Stanford (2002). A petition objecting to the selection of Condoleezza Rice as commencement speaker for Stanford graduation 2002. Available at http://www.stanford.edu/group/rats/condi/Condoleezza_ petition.html.

Reid, J. (2005). Bush's fixer: Condoleezza Rice has a history of covering for the Bush administration failures. Available at http://www.commondreams.org/ views05/0429–27.htm.

Rice, C. (2005, 21 March). Remarks to the press in China. Available at http:// www.state.gov/secretary/rm/2005/43678.htm.

Rice, C. (2005, 27 May). Address to the Commonwealth Club. Available at http://www.commonwealthclub.org/archive/05/05-05rice-speech.html.

Rice, C. (2005, 2 September). International relief activities related to hurricane Katrina. Available at http://www.state.gov/secretary/rm/2005/52478.htm.

Rice, C. (2005, 25 October). Interview on Canadian Broadcasting Corporation with Susan Bonner. Available at http://www.state.gov/secretary/ rm/2005/55576.htm.

Rice, C. (2004, 22 March). 9/11: For the record. *The Washington Post*, A21.

Rice, C. (2004, 8 April). Opening remarks to the National Commission on Terrorist Attacks upon the United States. Available at http://www.9-11commission.gov/ hearings/hearing9.rice_statement.pdf.

Rice, C. (2003, 23 January). Why we know Iraq is lying. Available at http://www. nytimes.com.

Rice, C. (2000). Campaign 2000: Promoting the national interest. Available at http://www.foreignaffairs.org.

Rice, C. (1984). *The Soviet Union and the Czechloslovak army 1948–1983: Uncertain allegiance*. Princeton, NJ: Princeton University Press.

Richmond, N. (2005). Letter from a black man in Canada: Rosa Parks vs. Condoleezza Rice. Available at http://www.blackcommentator. com/159/159_guest_parks_v_rice.html.

Robinson, E. (2005a, 23 October). Alabama's daughter: Returning to her roots from the mountaintop. *The Washington Post*, B07.

Robinson, E. (2005b, 25 October). Opinion: Alabama's daughter Condoleezza Rice. Available at http://www.washingtonpost.com/wp-dyn/content/ discussion/2005/10/24/DI2005102401345.html.

Russakoff, D. (2005, 6 February). Team Rice, playing away? Will State's head coach miss her first kickoff? Available at http://www.washingtonpost.com/ wp-dyn/articles/A1547–2005Feb5.html.

Russakoff, D. (2001, 6 September). Lessons of might and right. Available at http:// www.washingtonpost.com/wp-dyn/articles/A54664–2001Sep6.html.

Schwartz, T. (1997). Germany unified and Europe transformed: A study in state-craft. [Review] *The American Historical Review, 102 (1)*, 132.

Slavin, B. (2005, 1 December). Politics? Rice is focused on job she has now. Available at http://www.usatoday.com/news/washington/2005-12-01-rice-profile_x.htm.

Stanford University News Service (1991, 6 May). Back from D.C., Rice offers inside look at U.S.–Soviet relations. Available at http://www.stanford. edu/dept/news/pr/91/910506Arc1394.html.

Steins, L. (2003). *Colin Powell: A biography*. Westport, CT: Greenwood Press.

Stevenson, R. (2005, 12 November). Bush critics contend partisan critics hurt war effort. Available at http://www.nytimes.com/2005/11/12/politics/ 12bush.html?th&emc=th.

Stroebel, W. (2005, 6 December). Rice defends U.S. detainee policy. Available at http://www.mercurynews.com/mld/mercurynews/news/politics/13339112. htm.

Struck, D. (2005, 26 October). In Ottawa, Rice seeks to temper bitterness about Bush policies. *The Washington Post*, A10.

Suskind, R. (2004). *The price of loyalty: George W. Bush, the White House, and the education of Paul O'Neill*. New York: Simon & Schuster.

Tilove, J. (2005, 17 January). King's dream fulfilled in Condoleezza Rice? Available at http://archives.seattletimes.nwsource.com/cgi-bin/texis.cgi/web/vortex/ display?slug=mlkrice17&date=20050117.

Ullman, W. (1986). The Soviet Union and the Czechoslovak army, 1948–1983 (Review). *Russian Review, 45 (3)*, 313–314.

Wade, M. D. (2003). *Condoleezza Rice: Being the best*. Brookfield, CT: Millbrook Press.

Washington, B. T. (1901). *Up from slavery.* Chicago: Lushera Books.

Washington Post. (2000). Condoleezza Rice at the Republican National Convention. Available at http://www.washingtonpost.com/wp-srv/onpolitics/elections/ricetext080100.htm.

WBAI (2004, 25 August). U.S. makes unilateral call for regime change in Zimbabwe. Available at http://www.wbai.org/index.php?option=content&task=view&id=3376.

Wendland, J. (2005, 19 April). Condoleezza Rice orders scrapping of terrorism report. Available at http://www.commondreams.org/views05/0419–24.htm.

The White House (2004). National security advisor Condoleezza Rice opening remarks. The National Commission on Terrorist Attacks on the United States. Office of the Press Secretary. Available at http://www.9-11commission.gov/hearings/hearing9/rice_statement.pdf.

Woodward, B. (2002). *Bush at war.* New York: Simon & Schuster.

Wright, R., & Kessler, G. (2005, 31 July). At State, Rice takes control of diplomacy. Available at http://www.washingtonpost.com/wp-dyn/content/article/2005/07/30/AR2005073001081.html.

Wright, R., & Wilson, S. (2005, 16 November). Rice negotiates deal to open Gaza crossings. Available at http://www.washingtonpost.com/wp-dyn/content/article/2005/11/15/AR2005111500144.html.

Zelikow, P. & Rice, C. (1995). *Germany reunified and Europe transformed: A study in statecraft.* Cambridge, MA: Harvard University Press.

INDEX